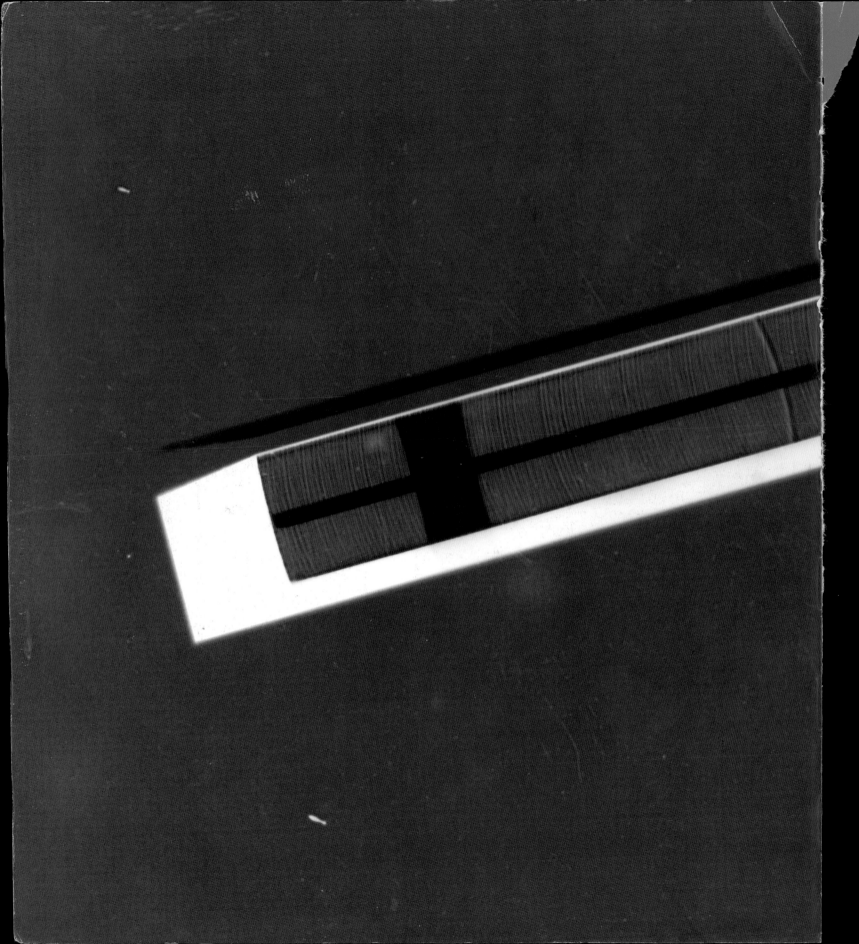

'. . . yes',

i said, for the first time and the end:

a moment within the moment,
a time preceding the last—
everything everyday in a month,
a moment,

thirty three years ;

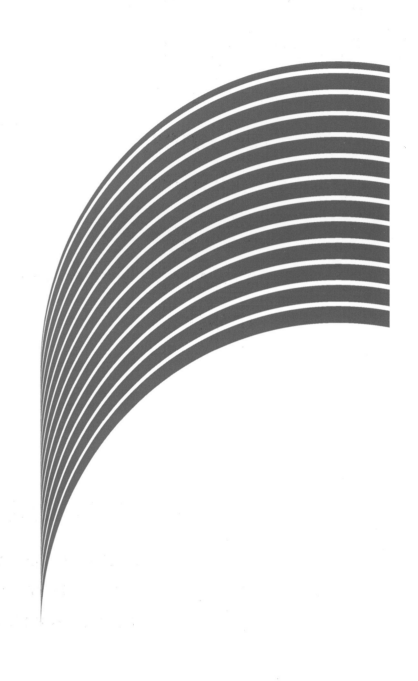

a train in motion,

leaving london,

power lines,

rail lines,

a red rusted tower on ridge on its own:

markings,

distance.

bridges.

places with trees,
flat space,
distance—

a baby in white touching its reflection—

inside,

still,

moving,
a sequence,

houses and roads,

leaving behind.

a child keeps crying and i smell bananas.
my joints ache.
sitting on a stone stile.

sitting under a dome looking out, holding still:

the man who sang songs with stones was stolen before he was born;
he lived all his life under the hiding bridge. the song the stones sang was about beginning.
the song sang about itself.
his arrangements were so pure and so cold that they could freeze the warmest heart.

the stones' skins were polished words that showed him pictures of lost

things.

the hiding bridge was a place where no one could be alone or concealed.
one of the songs was the story of an old man who was near death and needed a friend;
so he wrote her a contract and signed it,
and she was near by until he died.

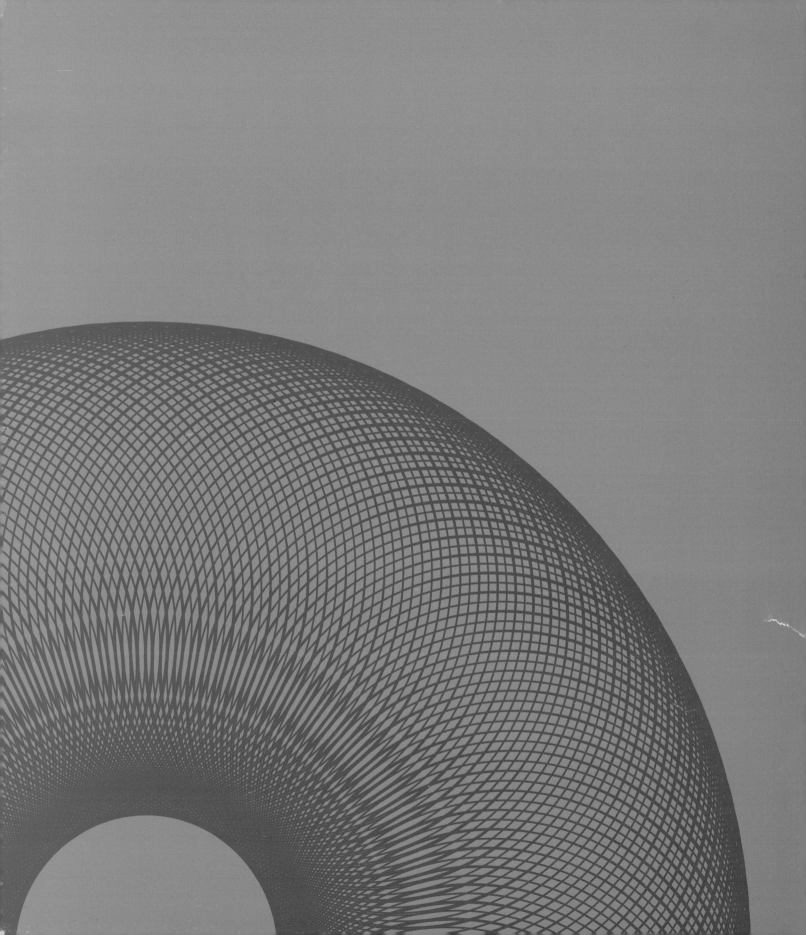

first found valley

who goes where spoken wonders come?

walked upon

lost to the world

arriving

and now

uncovered

the waiting

far shale

rolling   a city

the walls   and all

hidden under pages of stone

a shake   a shake

—grey

ending

known

—gold

yellow lay the easy waters

revealed

movement to become shadow : weigh   i know

you know

then the silence will rise

from

my dreams   yellow lay the easy waters

yellow lay the easy waters

and in speaking

there are some things

i can't describe

we take off down a slip road, a long way
away, like a rustling or a flickering, we take
off down river, swinging. now we're
together. this is ancient electricity,
microscopic fountains of light, assembled, she
squeezing energy from the air:

walks in
patterns,
makes the
sound of
falling leaves. born together again,
we're liquid and light,
and she is all about this moment and knows there isn't anything else and that's what she always reminds me of.

when still,

circles

are courses for stories—a story for
every moment, two small puddles
beside a drain.
when still **circles**

wheel within wheeling

circles

—the semi-

circle will,

a twisting world; when the very first
word in the universe spells the human
and the real lesson so rarely learnt—
still unwillingly, speaking, seeking the
long lost substance out of these days

and the previous years **,**

separate, the spring has been sealed with the colour i forgot—

the colour, the roots of the sea and
the forest's waves:

here,
now here,
the colour of the sea:

here,

now here

lies the sea,

the sea that is only sea,
the sea of the world below time at the centre of questions,

wandering and ill, new steps without waking, *sleeping,*

like the day of the sea,

waves of time cover you and me through shorter and shorter days—

set the course for the coming years,

the urge that fills the sails;

set the course of the coming years from here,

now here,

lies the sea—

the first man and the sea and the universe.

sorrow is stranger than the sea,
and stranger and as sad;

how often in recent times i've

been

thinking

of you as my myths root,

strange that sorrow that tongueless ages and the strong strange sea softly survives,
surfaced around sunrise on a summer day,

drying the streets beneath the sea,

when my myth becomes your history:

how often i'll think of you.

so now is now,

and now begins,

and the sea's vague rising sings the singer who taught our lips to move,
whose voice was heard before the wind—

the moment will come,

but when?

and then?

and then

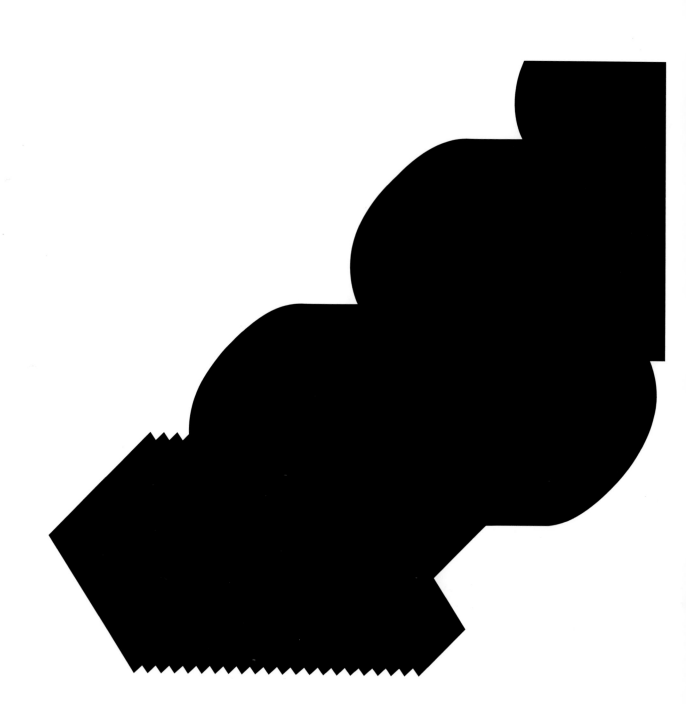

strange feeling—
one age to the next. from out of the airless:
the nothing that can't be explained,
has no name,
not the idea of names—
no temperature—
there is music there—
shapes describe hanging changes still and free,
sound of going and of sadness,
        a sad word,

thought and action multiplying
circles echo of each other faith rising
tracing a pattern that is never drawn
or repeated without transforming
again and again to live and stand
outside itself in a spirit

this is work—
sight,
lines:
inheritance,
from one thing to the next asking—
what is my nature?
what is the nature of the thing?
a difference:
an act of honesty builds towers and gardens we can only pass by in silence.

a mirror in an empty room reflects a seven starred constellation.

at the edge of a small

wood, near a hut, a

white feather falls into a

rain-water puddle.

a few days ago i took some cress seeds and sowed my name with them.
and it came up right pretty.

and it made me so happy that i can hardly say.

and yesterday when i came back from boating somebody had come into the garden and stepped on my name.
i cried for a long time.
i am going to sow the bed again.

transcribed from 'The Enigma of Kaspar Hauser'
written and directed by Werner Herzog, 1974

don't you hear anything,
don't you hear the terrible voice that cries across the horizon,

Silence?

the voice that people usually call

since i have been living in this silent valley i hear it always,
it does not let me sleep.

George Buchner
The Complete Plays, p.270
Methuen 1987

———

your name is a bell that holds me responsible

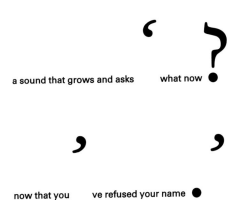

a sound that grows and asks   what now ●

now that you   ve refused your name ●

there are some places that could be anywhere:
there aren't many days when i don't go on a bus or a train.
this is where things are in these uncountable days:
removed words,   now this day has barely chased the night away ●
pushing at their meaning,
dumb with the settled sense of arrival.

everyone has the same story to tell.

everyone has a story to tell.

there aren't the words—our judgement defeats us.
what happens when and what happens then;
crystal life unconscious even of the unconscious decisions it never made;
a home in the jar,
a place that could be anywhere.

●

a new sense ●

,

suspended away,
even—
what would it be like?
the silk rope has been cut and i   m drifting ,

we'd have to open our eyes.
we dream of things we never believe.
becalmed ● all of these things have happened:

———

flooded days,
bring me to my knees   sleight of hand,
ease—
behind your eyes are more tears than you've ever shed;
,   they suspend on the day,
touch one place and another—
the forest and the lake,
the field and the sea—
sometimes it   s more than enough to bend with the wind ●
lights span and multiply from season into day.

on a line,
a point to a point,
when the day began ,   a point and a line.
these things have all happened—
● journey,
and you appeared ● circle,
wheel—
these have all happened.

now ,
, what is the shape of a road?
its curves get lost—

i   m certain ●

———

how the tide of life

flows ●

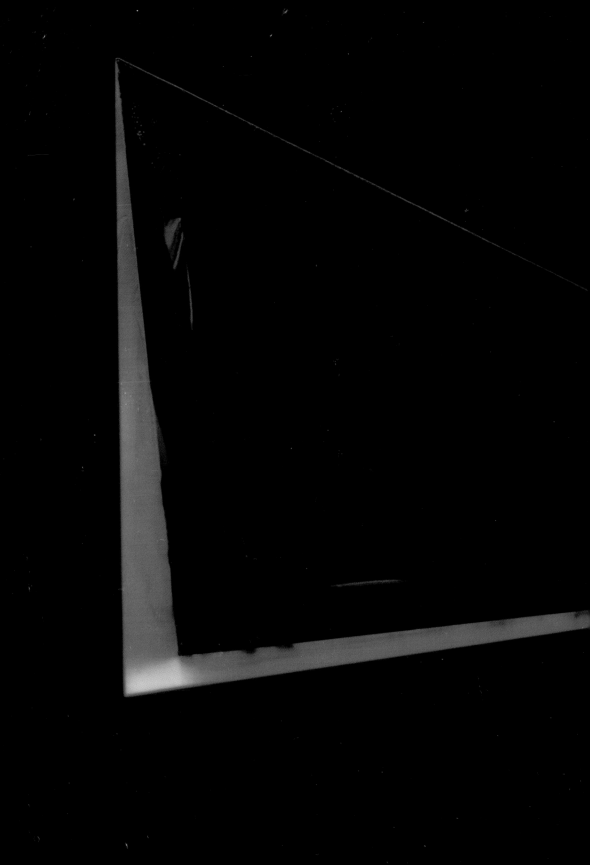

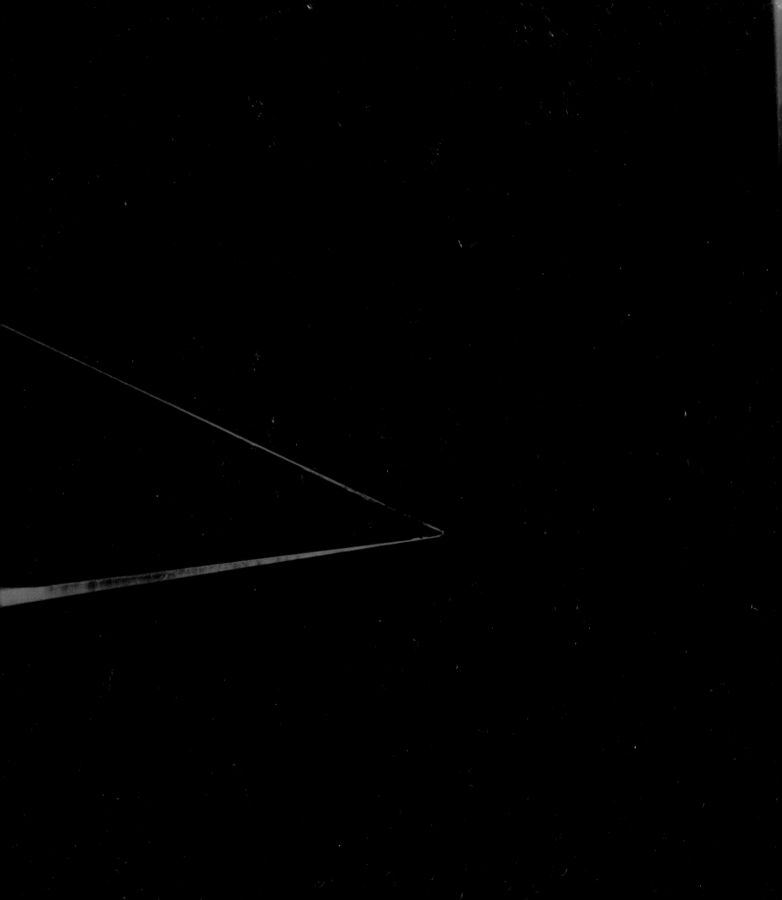

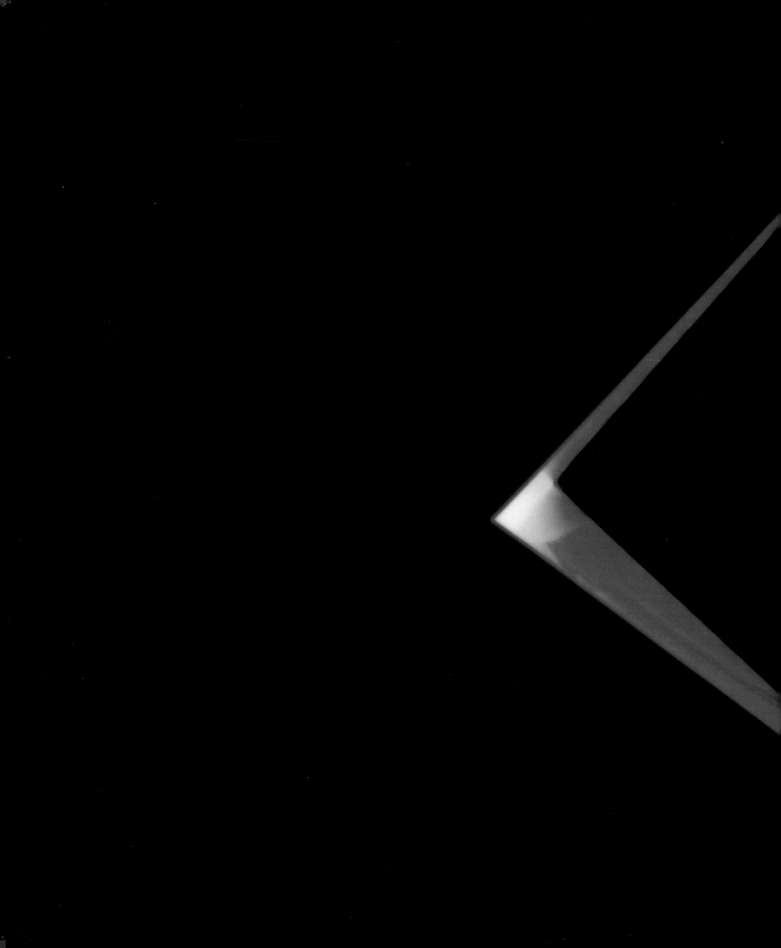

seasons and signs ●

the image of a sleeping world ●

don't look back—
the shape of a road—
in such a short time—

evolution,

seasons and signs ●
this time.

well,
i've picked this up again and it always gives me a thread,
another set of links from moment to moment.
navigating the solitary summits above memory ●
this is a last time—
every moment filled with moving,
and they're gone,
moments out of time,
these seasons run this whole life through

mistfalls unclutched.

this is what these are,
moments and shapes,
speed and slow time—

another sun comes ❟

such a small love,
like a carnival of thought—
a slow train stopped—
some remain,
some disappear.
the speed of slow time and the snow,

another sun goes ●

●

there is one demand i'll make of you ●

treat me as your self ●

,

as another day ends you say you   ll tell me tomorrow ,

and the game continues ●

i can't wait ●

the density of thought and the sparse years.
nature again.
it's all there,
in my leaves and the leaves on the trees:

?
why have we lost ●

?
which possibilities did we throw away ●

fixed to a place and a day,
the abstract and the real—
they explain each other.

waiting outside under an umbrella in a street with other people waiting and the sky is grey.
just now i waited to look after something for someone else.
now i'm waiting and they're late—
and i'd rushed to be here.
i'm annoyed.

and then it goes away.

breaking with the habit of a lifetime inactive reduction crippling—

these wings are all i have to give to you ●

a day,
like no other,
with marshes lit brown grey with etched lines,
a night of the fifth season with no rain,
and a drowned sunken garden with swimming birds;

sunlight dips and flares from minute to minute **,**

i've lost my way in this word—
a list of things i've known,
a new kind of friend revealed by the things i do.
this change is too much;
lies from loved ones every day,
and now i'm doing it,
too,
beginning to—
days of broken lines.

a curtain curled open shows rows of bricks ●

new days,
new shapes— **,**   **,**
a new colour,
a new sense.

i can   t help feeling you   re living for a love you never knew

singing,
sing music that can say everything,

,   **,**   'over the rooftops',

saying everything without speaking,

travelling without moving:
i can   t stop believing you   re crying for the paper world you say surrounds you

emanation.

that you say has given you all you ever knew ●

,   **,**

of all the places on the earth we   ll never see and the places we   ll see again ●   ●   ●

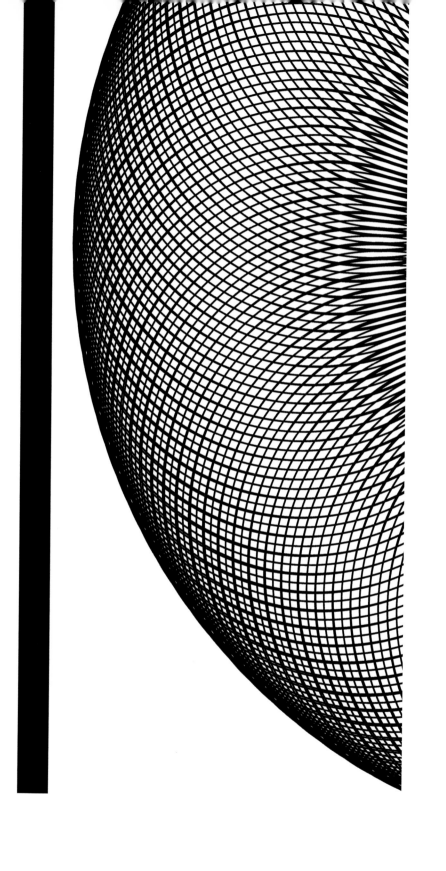

when the stars lived beneath the earth there was a moment of silence ●

the hallway, the staircase **,**

———

the room

,

a train journey i   d never take begins again as i fade from view from you and your other winter **,**

the fifth season that sees the sky drain over marshes lit with etched lines ●

of these rooftops there are too many stories to be sung and cried **,**

while the speed that beats us down quickens with each staggering day ●

the vacuum of our selves will be filled with angels' breath ●

long ago *,*

lost *,* •

evermore •

the tongue i know we must have had one day *,*

gave way in change for these sights that sting *,*

acid rising from the usual nighttime ache into my throat *,*

⎯⎯⎯⎯⎯

asks 'which is the same?'

here is the sea *,*

again •

the thing can't come *,*

or won't *,*

or comes unformed *,*

stilling strain goes on *,*

goes on storm shadowed *,*

mute mind lingering locked in slight words *,*

standing fallow *,*

palms upturned *,*

disbelieving •

awakening,

the immediate second

a velvet morning suspended in one breath.

breathe out—

with every moment

existence for a moment as an emanation—

sparked with friction

a circle on a circle,

every little flash

not a point on a line.

spreading as a stain of light

i am inside out for half my life.

the spring grass grows but it doesn't know how:

overlapping all the time

in the spaces between the letters punctured with rain,

in the shining blank page,

proceeding from the first unknown

on the stairs,

at a desk,

and unknowable cause

on a holiday,

affecting effect

again,

'from day to day'.

history is a slip of the tongue,

another game.

nothing can be said

everyone has a new story to tell.

nothing needs to be done

nothing is that simple

komplje

down the road,
just to the right,
second one,
there,
there,

by that beat,
that's where and what it is,
i'll be there shortly,
i mean in a while,
we'll have a drink and you'll tell me,
just tell me,
what sense is that and that was there as i launched out in my little shuttleship space,
when it was seven years on and it had all come true,

yes,
it had,
don't believe me but it came true—

we are all

everything at once
all the time everywhere:

no thought,
no logic,
no attachment,
no leaving,
no sense,
no senses,
no looking,
no searching,
no finding,
no nothing,
no something,
no word,
no yes,
no no,

the questions you're asking
are the wrong ones.

and then,
you were already perfect.

here we are,

and now,

here she comes,
like something in the air calling, and she asks me, and

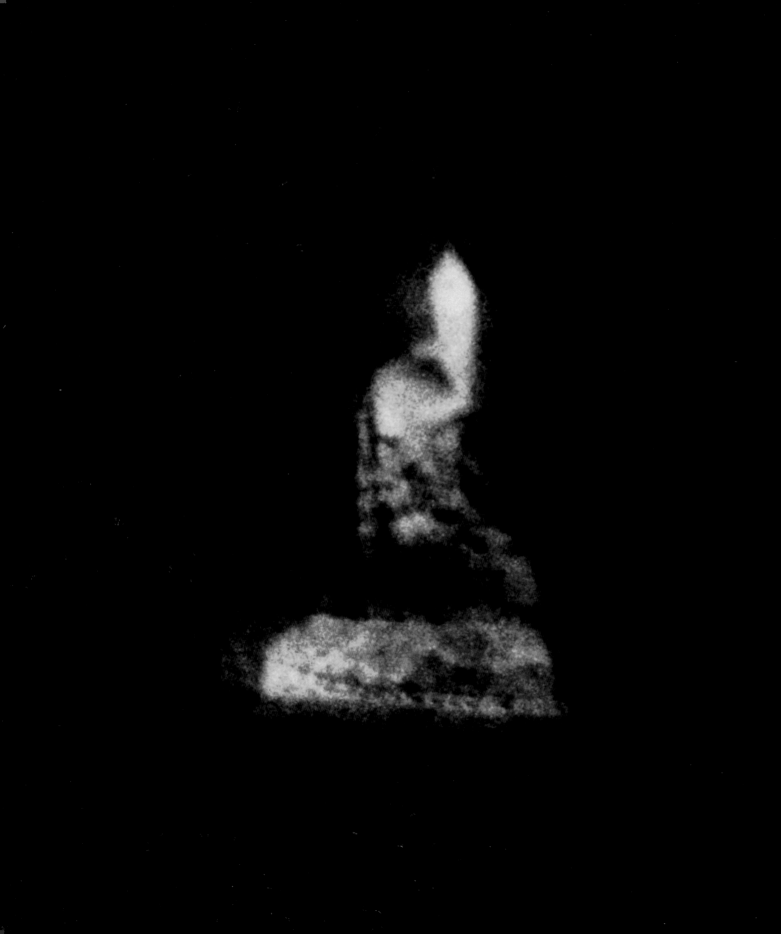

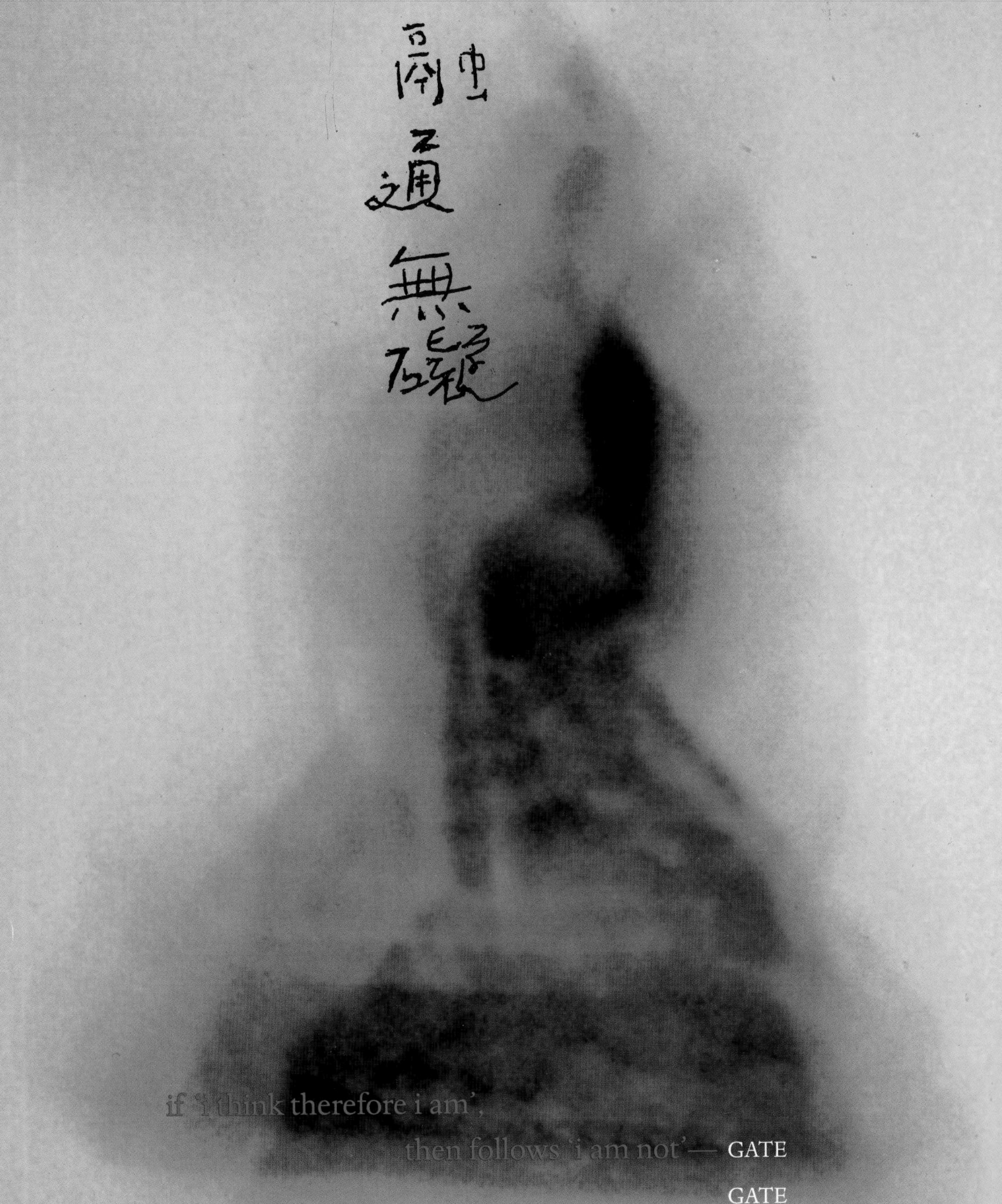

if 'i think therefore i am',

then follows 'i am not' — GATE

GATE

PARAGATE

PARASAMGATE

BODHI SVAHA

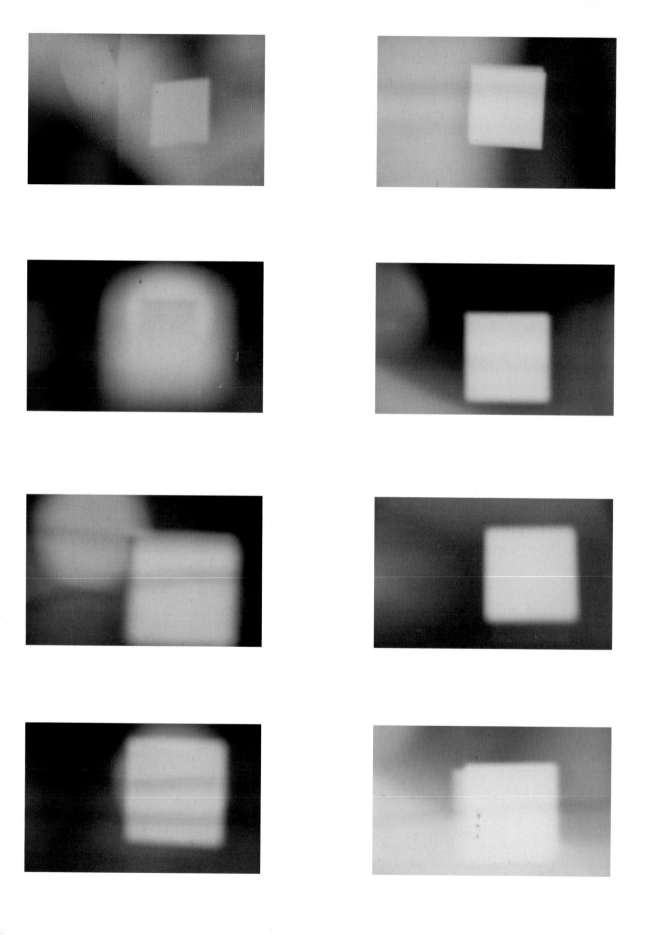

ROBIN LAME SCATTANTI

SIXTIES SOUL FUNK BLACK CONSCIOUSNESS LYRICS

LEON THOMAS

THE SLOW MOTION SEQUENCES OF SKI JUMPING IN THE GREAT ECSTASY OF THE WOODCARVER STEIN, A SHORT FILM BY WERNER HERZOG.

SHE IS WEARING A SILVERY BLACK
KNEE LENGTH LEATHER EFFECT
COAT. SHE IS CHEWING GUM, SHE IS
ATTRACTIVE. HER DARK BROWN HAIR
FALLS AROUND HER SHOULDERS IN
TIGHT CORKSCREW RINGLETS, IT
APPEARS TO BE WET, BUT IT IS NOT
(IT IS A HAIR PRODUCT DESIGNED
TO GIVE THIS EXACT EFFECT). SHE
IS WEARING DARK RED/BROWN
LIPSTICK, AND BLACK NAIL VARNISH.
SHE IS WEARING TIGHT BEIGE SHINY
TROUSERS THAT ARE SLIGHTLY
FLARED AT THE ANKLE, AND BLACK
LEATHER ROUND TOED PLATFORM
BOOTS.

LA PRINCESS LEIA ET SON SPEEDER BIKE

DON'T MISUNDERSTAND ME, I USED TO BE A REAL FAN, BUT BACK THEN IN EIGHTY SIX I SHARED A CELL WITH THE GODFATHER OF FUNK – JAMES BROWN. HE WAS REALLY VERY CLUMSY WALKING INTO STUFF, THINGS LIKE THAT, AND SHOUTING REALLY LOUD LIKE ON HIS RECORDS.

LANDO EN GARDE DE JABBA

QUICK EVOKE AN ALTERNATIVE WORLD.

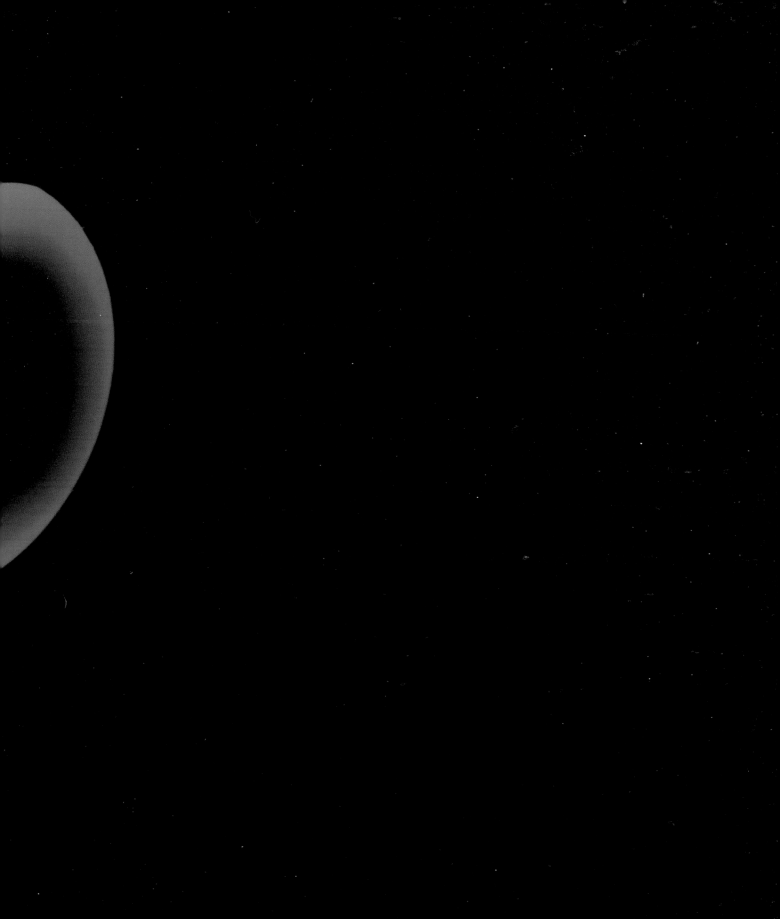

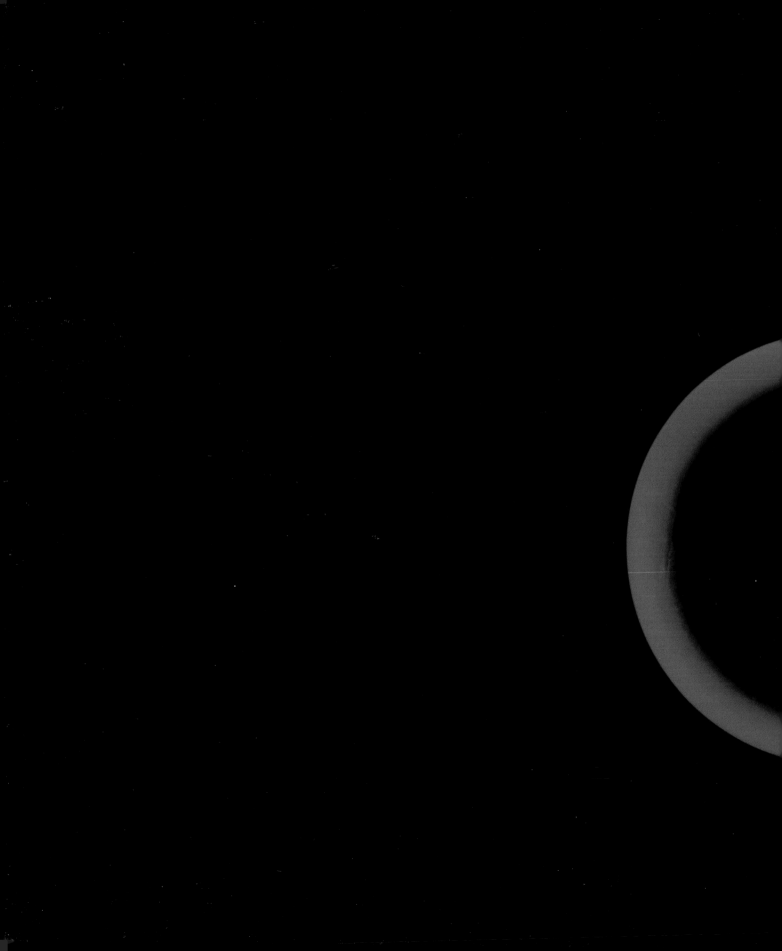

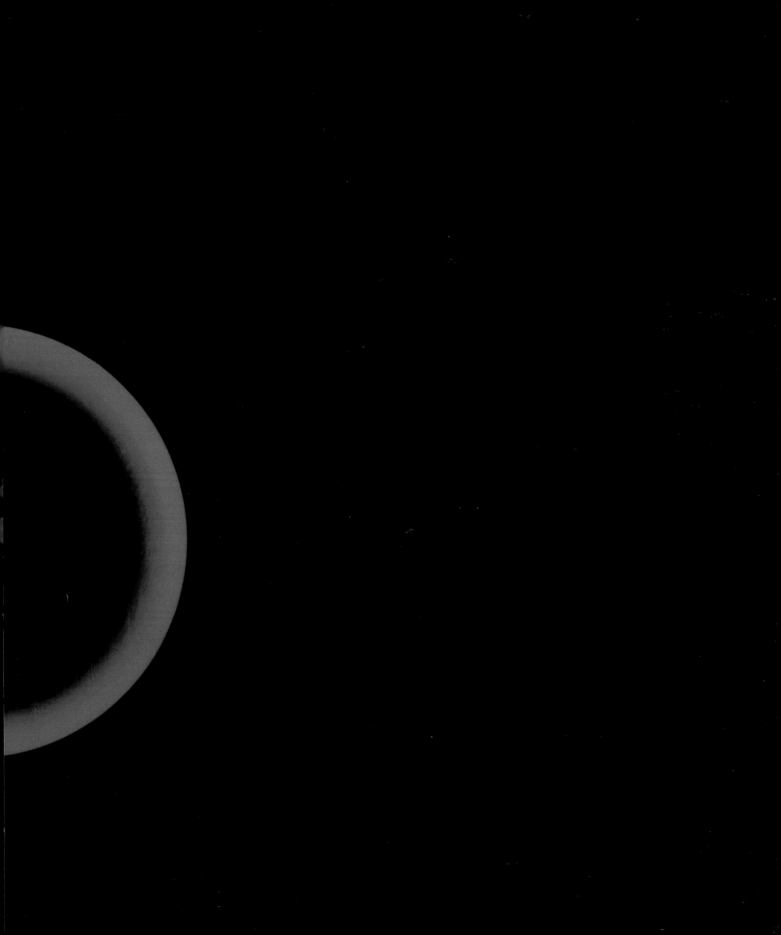

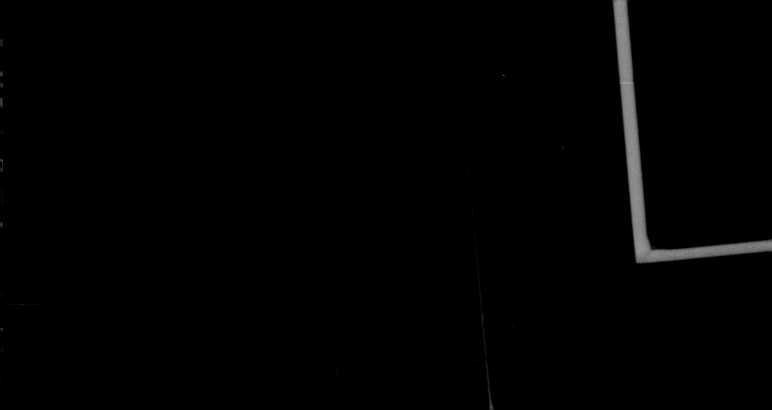

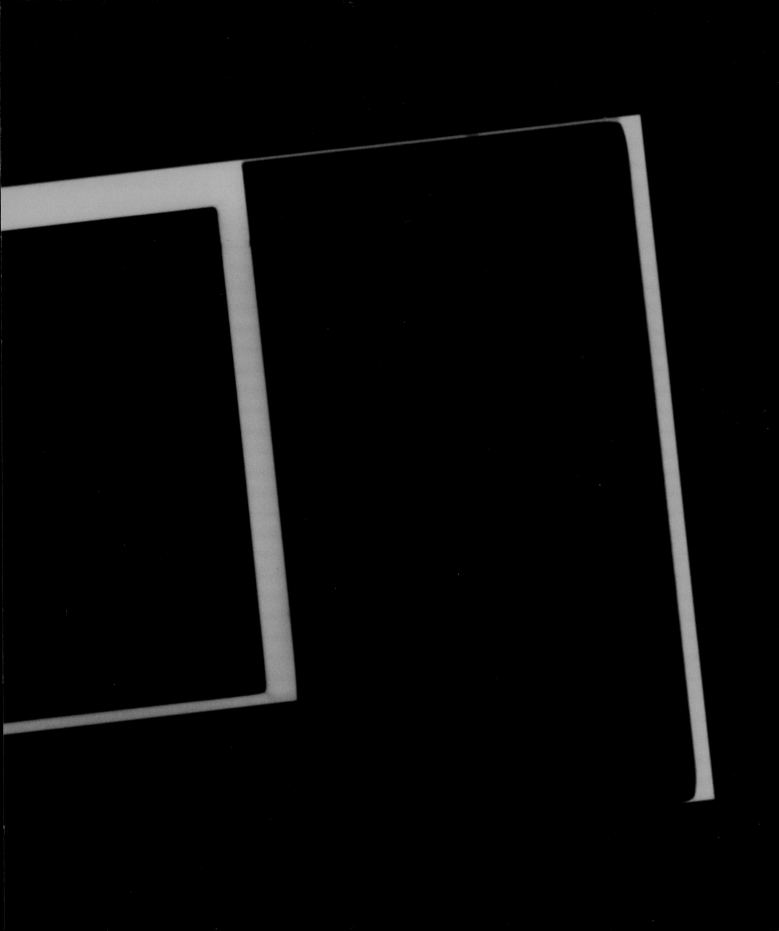

WHEN THE FIRST BULLET STRUCK, IT PASSED
QUICKLY THROUGH MY CHEST AND OUT OF MY
BACK, MORE OR LESS IN A STRAIGHT LINE.
WHAT SURPRISED ME WAS THE SMELL OF MY FLESH
BURNING AND HOW THE HEAT GENERATED BY THE
SPINNING BULLET AS IT PASSED THROUGH ME
RADIATED OUTWARDS IN A PERFECT CIRCLE SIMILAR
TO A PEBBLE THAT IS DROPPED INTO A STILL POND.
EACH WAVE AS IT MOVED FURTHER FROM ITS
SOURCE CARRIED SLIGHTLY LESS HEAT THAN THE
WAVE BEFORE IT.
AS I FELT THE FINAL WAVE OF HEAT REACH MY
STOMACH, NECK AND BICEP FROM THE FIRST
BULLET, I BECAME AWARE OF THE SECOND, THIRD
AND FOURTH BULLET STRIKING ME.
THE SECOND PASSED THROUGH MY ABDOMEN,
EXITING BENEATH MY LEFT KIDNEY
THE THIRD STRUCK MY NECK AND SEEMED TO TAKE
A LONG TIME BEFORE EXITING JUST BELOW MY
RIGHT EAR (I COULD ACTUALLY HEAR IT SPINNING
AS IT PASSED CLOSE TO MY EAR).

THE FOURTH HIT MY LEG JUST BENEATH MY HIP
CAUSING ME TO FALL, MY LEG BENDING
INVOLUNTARILY AT THE KNEE THE ... ING
CUT THROUGH CONNECTING FIBR... BONE AND MUSCLE.
AGAIN I BECAME AWARE OF THE BEAUTIFUL
ALMOST PERFECT CIRCULAR WAVES OF HEAT
GENERATED OUTWARDS BY THE RAPIDLY SPINNING
BULLETS AS THEY PASSED THROUGH ME
WHEN THE WAVES OF HEAT FROM TWO SEPARATE
BULLET WOUNDS CROSSED ONE ANOTHER IT WAS
SOMETHING VERY SPECIAL, STRANGELY
COMFORTING LIKE FEELING BATHED BY THE
WARMTH OF A NUMBER OF DISTANT SUNS
CONTAINED WITHIN ONE'S BODY.
I REALISED I WAS NOW SITTING ON THE FLOOR, MY
HAND WET AND RESTING IN A POOL OF MY OWN
BLOOD. I BEGAN TO FEEL TIRED AND I SLOWLY
LOWERED MYSELF ONTO MY ELBOW AND RESTING
MY HEAD ON MY SHOULDER I CLOSED MY EYES.

I ONCE SAW A WHITE LIGHT IS AS WHAT
SEEMED TO BE AN EXTREMELY LARGE
AMOUNT OF WHITE LIGHT IN AN
EXTREMELY SHORT AMOUNT OF TIME
THE AMOUNT OF LIGHT IN THE AMOUNT
OF TIME IS SIGNIFICANT.
THE MEANING OF THE WHITE LIGHT I
COULD NOT FULLY EXPLAIN.

TWO WHITE MIDDLECLASS WELL BALANCED AND HAPPY INDIVIDUALS MOVE TOWARDS TRAGEDY AS DRUG ADDICTS AND GANGSTERS.

A BLACK GUY JOINS A CIRCUS AS A CLOWN TO ESCAPE THE TRAGEDY OF HIS LIFE (HE SUFFERED MENTAL ABUSE AS A CHILD). AND BECOMES DEPRESSED BY THE EVERYDAY RACISM OF LIVING IN LONDON. HIS ROLE AS A CLOWN SEEMS TO MAKE HIS TRAGEDY MORE COMPLETE.

two parallel white lines, each measuring twelve miles long, drawn in the sky each line starting from the earth's surface and moving upwards at a thirty degree angle.

THERE WAS A WHITE LIGHT. THERE SEEMED TO BE AN EXTREME AMOUNT OF WHITE LIGHT IN AN EXTREMELY SHORT AMOUNT OF TIME. THE AMOUNT OF LIGHT IN THE AMOUNT OF TIME WAS SIGNIFICANT. THE MEANING OF THE WHITE LIGHT I COULD NOT FULLY EXPLAIN.

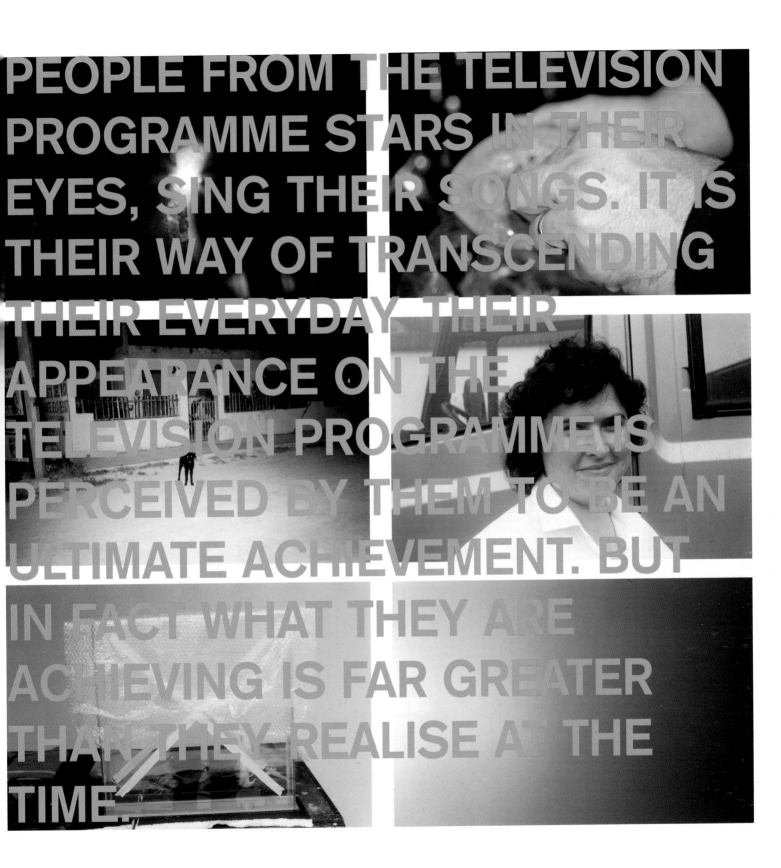

PEOPLE FROM THE TELEVISION PROGRAMME STARS IN THEIR EYES, SING THEIR SONGS. IT IS THEIR WAY OF TRANSCENDING THEIR EVERYDAY. THEIR APPEARANCE ON THE TELEVISION PROGRAMME IS PERCEIVED BY THEM TO BE AN ULTIMATE ACHIEVEMENT. BUT IN FACT WHAT THEY ARE ACHIEVING IS FAR GREATER THAN THEY REALISE AT THE TIME.

THE HUMAN BEING BEGINS TO DIVIDE, AT FIRST SPLITTING INTO TWO EQUAL PARTS. THESE TWO PARTS CONTINUE TO DIVIDE CREATING FOUR, EIGHT, SIXTEEN, THIRTY TWO, SIXTY FOUR INDEPENDENT UNITS. THIS CONTINUAL DIVIDING OCCURS UNTIL EACH INDIVIDUAL UNIT REACHES INFINITY. INFINITY IS A STATE MEANING ENDLESS TIME SPACE OR QUANTITY.

I WAS WALKING DOWN THE ROAD YESTERDAY, WHEN I SAW A BABY ROLL OUT OF ITS PRAM, AND INTO THE PATH OF A SPEEDING MOTOR CAR. I DIVED IN FRONT OF THE CAR PUSHING THE BABY TO ONE SIDE. ALL FOUR WHEELS OF THE CAR WENT OVER MY BACK, BUT I WASN'T HURT, THE BABY WAS FINE.

HE STOOD IN FRONT OF ME, AND I MOVED EFFORT
LESSLY TOWARDS HIM. ALL COLOUR SUBSTITUTED BY
AN INFRA RED GLOW, SOUND CONTAINED AND DISTANT.
MY HAND AND ARM MOVED SLOWLY TOWARDS HIS
FACE. MY FIST, FOREARM, ELBOW, SHOULDER, MY
WHOLE BODY TIGHTENED, SOLIDIFYING AS IT CAME
INTO CONTACT WITH HIS LIPS. I SEEMED TO MOVE
THROUGH HIM. FROM HIS MOUTH INDIVIDUAL BLOOD
CELLS FLEW IN ULTRA SLOW MOTION, SUSPENDED AND
SPINNING THROUGH A SPACE JUST ABOVE MY
FOREARM, A MINIATURE GALAXY. SMALL FRAGMENTS OF
TOOTH FALLING FASTER THAN THE BLOOD CELLS
BOUNCED OFF MY SHIRTSLEEVE AND DISAPPEARED
FROM MY FIELD OF VIEW. THE FORCE OF CONTACT HAD
KNOCKED HIM BACK 20 FEET OR SO. AGAIN I MOVED
TOWARDS HIM. HE SEEMED DISORIENTATED, HE ASKED
ME WHO HIT HIM, AND FEIGNING SYMPATHY, I
ANSWERED THAT I WAS NOT SURE. AGAIN I BROUGHT
MY FIST HARD INTO HIS FACE, HIS HEAD FLEW BACK-
WARDS AND HE FELL TO THE FLOOR ARCING THROUGH
THE DARK SPACE, I KNELT OVER HIM, I COULD SEE HE
HAD NOTHING MORE TO GIVE. I MOVED AWAY.

BATMAN IS AT THE BEACH.

HE IS SNORKELLING

WITH ROBIN IN THE SEA.

A CROSS-EYED DUCK. A CARTOON DOG DRESSED AS A PRIEST. A STAG ASLEEP IN A CHAIR LAUGHS ALOUD.

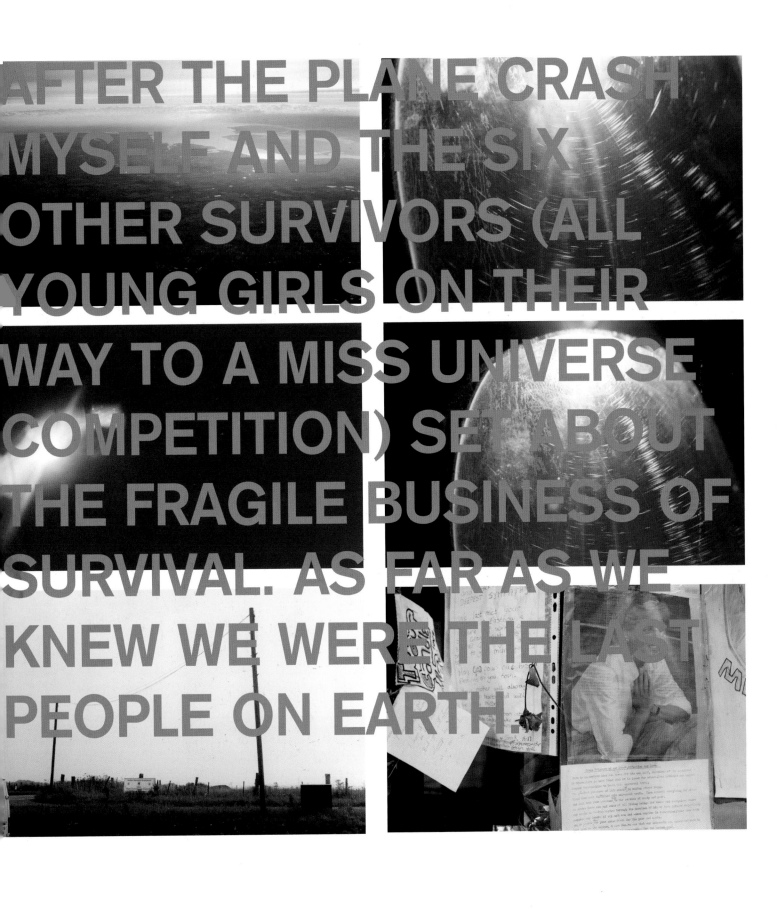

AFTER THE PLANE CRASH MYSELF AND THE SIX OTHER SURVIVORS (ALL YOUNG GIRLS ON THEIR WAY TO A MISS UNIVERSE (COMPETITION) SET ABOUT THE FRAGILE BUSINESS OF SURVIVAL. AS FAR AS WE KNEW WE WERE THE LAST PEOPLE ON EARTH.

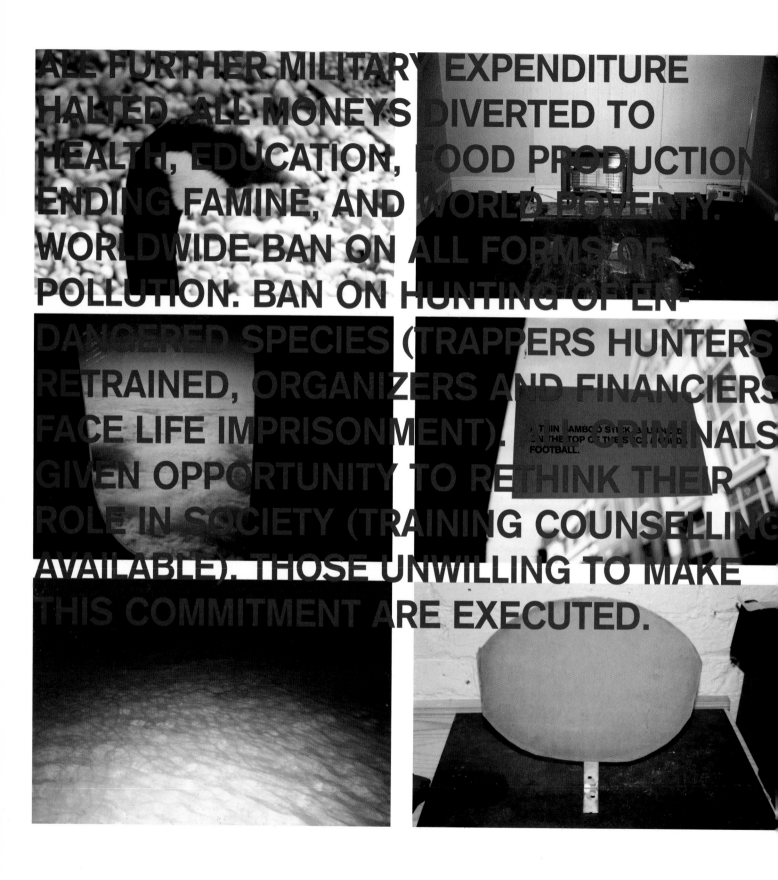

ALL FURTHER MILITARY EXPENDITURE HALTED. ALL MONEYS DIVERTED TO HEALTH, EDUCATION, FOOD PRODUCTION ENDING FAMINE, AND WORLD POVERTY. WORLDWIDE BAN ON ALL FORMS OF POLLUTION. BAN ON HUNTING OF ENDANGERED SPECIES (TRAPPERS HUNTERS RETRAINED, ORGANIZERS AND FINANCIERS FACE LIFE IMPRISONMENT). CRIMINALS GIVEN OPPORTUNITY TO RETHINK THEIR ROLE IN SOCIETY (TRAINING COUNSELLING AVAILABLE). THOSE UNWILLING TO MAKE THIS COMMITMENT ARE EXECUTED.

A GIRL WITH BLONDE HAIR. HER WORDS COME OUT OF HER NECK.

A NONSENSICAL BALLAD SUNG WITH HEART BY A BAD SINGER. THE SUBJECT MATTER THUS ABSTRACTED BECOMES TRANSCENDENTAL.

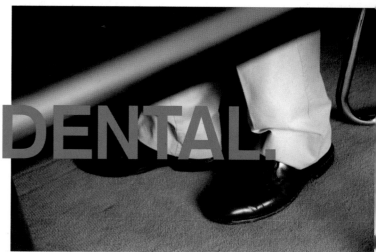

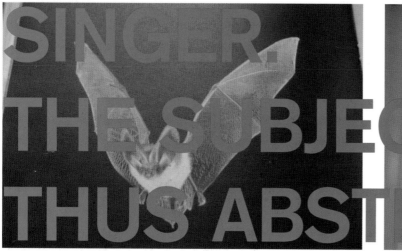

WE KISSED AND A LITTLE RAINBOW BRIDGE APPEARED IN FRONT OF MY FACE. SPARKLING DOE, RABBITS, SMALL CARTOON BIRDS SAT AMONGST LARGE FLOWERS. A BLUE SKY WITH WHITE CLOUDS FLOATED ABOVE... AND THEN THEY WERE GONE IN A FLASH. THE TASTE OF HER MOUTH AND HER BREATH'S SOFTNESS EXPLODED EVERYTHING INSIDE OF ME. I BECAME A GALAXY OF SPARKLING DUST.

A CYLINDRICAL CONTAINER. A CLEAR LIQUID. THE LIQUID CLINGS TO THE OUTER EDGE OF THE CONTAINER.

THE BALLAD AS INTER-
PRETED BY BIG YOUTH.
TOUCH ME IN THE
MORNING IS ESPECIALLY
GOOD. ITS DISTORTION
SERVES TO MAKE IT
POIGNANT, AND SOME-
HOW MORE FRAGILE.

NEITHER FILM NOR LIFE

MY QUEST IS
THROUGH MEMORY
MY HAND AND ITS
FIVE FINGERS ARE
FIVE PATHS, A DECK
OF CARDS, A BELL,
GOLD.

I SAW YESTERDAY, ON MY WAY TO WORK, AN OLD LADY WHO APPEARED TO BE IN SOME DISTRESS. TWELVE YOUTHS, SOME ARMED WITH KNIVES, HAD SURROUNDED HER. ONE OF THE YOUTHS HELD THE OLD LADY BY HER WRIST. I WALKED TOWARDS HIM, AND HE PLUNGED HIS KNIFE AT MY CHEST. I TOOK HOLD OF HIS HAND, SNAPPED IT FORWARD AGAINST ITS JOINT, HIS WRIST BROKE AND HE DROPPED HIS KNIFE. KEEPING HOLD OF HIS HAND I ROTATED IT THROUGH 180 DEGREES, PULLED IT STRAIGHT THEN PUSHED IT SUDDENLY HARD AGAINST ITS JOINT. THE BONE SHEARED, A SHARPENED POINT PIERCED THROUGH HIS SKIN, BETWEEN THE ELBOW AND WRIST.

LINDEN ARDEN STOLE THE HIGHLIGHTS.

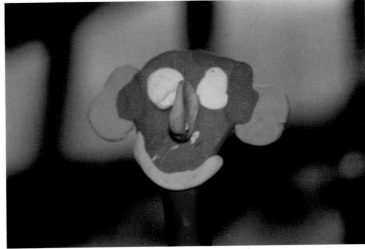

THE WORDS MOVE TOWARDS ME. THEY APPEAR TO BE MADE OF LIGHT. ON CLOSE EXAMINATION THEY HAVE NO APPARENT STRUCTURE, THEY PULSE AND GLOW UNEVENLY. EACH WORD HAS A SEPARATE MEANING. THIS MEANING SEEMS TO CREATE AROUND ITSELF ITS OWN INDIVIDUAL SPACE. THE SPACES THUS CREATED ARE DIFFERENT IN SIZE, SHAPE, COLOUR, AND APPEAR MORE DISTINCT AS THE WORDS WITHIN THEM BEGIN TO FADE. THESE INDIVIDUAL SPACES CONNECT TOGETHER AND FORM A LARGER MORE COMPLEX THREE DIMENSIONAL FORM.

A SMALL CUBE RESTING IN THE PALM OF A HAND, THE CUBE IS LIGHT BLUE IN COLOUR.

THEIR FEET MOVED SLOWLY PROPELLING THEM ABOVE THE TREE TOPS. IN THEIR HANDS THEY HELD SWORDS, SUNLIGHT ON STRIKING THE SHARPENED EDGE OF A BLADE WOULD EVOKE SONG. THE SONG OF EACH BLADE WAS DIFFERENT, THE SONG OF EACH BLADE HAD THE ABILITY TO PENETRATE FLESH.

A PERSON SUFFERS PAIN THAT RADICALLY CHANGES THEM. (THEY CHANGE IN ORDER TO SURVIVE). THE PERSON THEN ATTEMPTS TO REGAIN THAT PART OF THEM THAT WAS LOST.

AT THE POINT OF DEATH THE HUMAN BEING ATTEMPTS TO CHANGE FORM OR STATE. MANY ARE SUCCESSFUL SOME FOR EXAMPLE BECOME LIGHT OR COLOUR, SOME MAY TURN INTO SOUND, OTHERS MAY BECOME BIRDS OR MOTHS

I felt like floating,
I became a little crazy, but I want to stay here forever.
I could not see your face but I felt close to you.
I will not lose.

I feel "now".
I was attacked by strange senses.
I felt good.
It touched an unexpected point, I was shocked.
My head became empty, a strange feeling.
The silence when all stops. Words, meaning and everything
become as one and sometimes everything is meaningless.
Loneliness in a sensual city.
As everybody says "I felt very strange".
Light, sound, darkness, air. Everything embraces me.
I wanted to die.
I became dizzy.
Unconsciously I overlapped my view within the city,
An amusement park of words.

Poem by 12,700 people. Tokyo city, 1997.

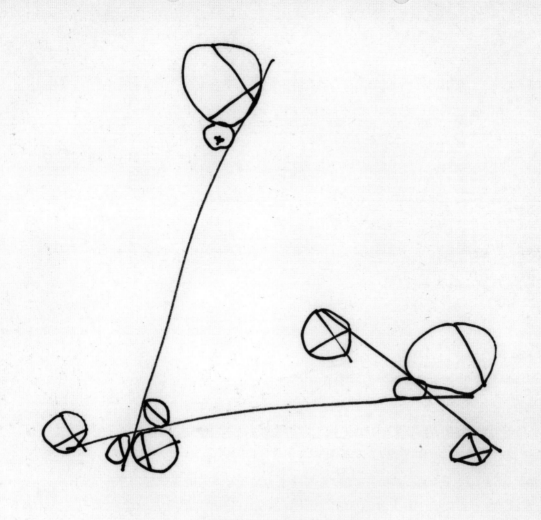

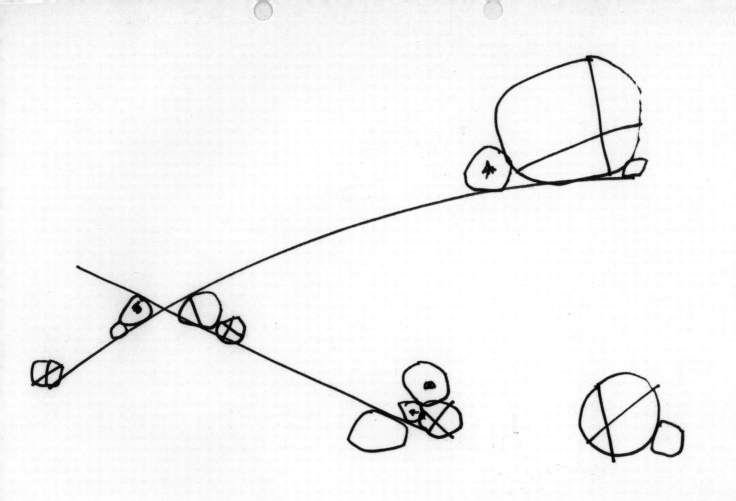

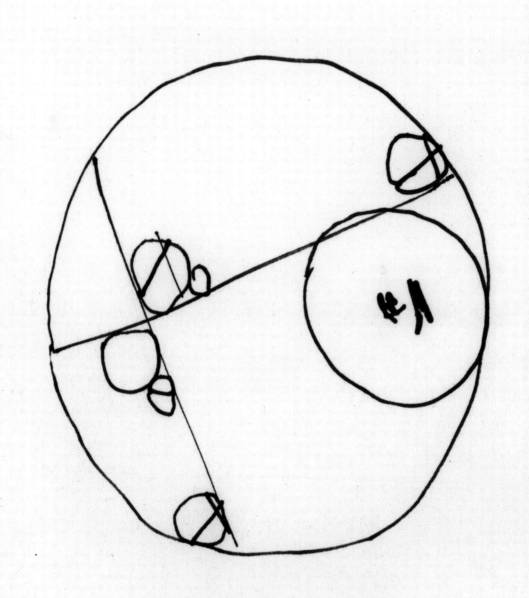

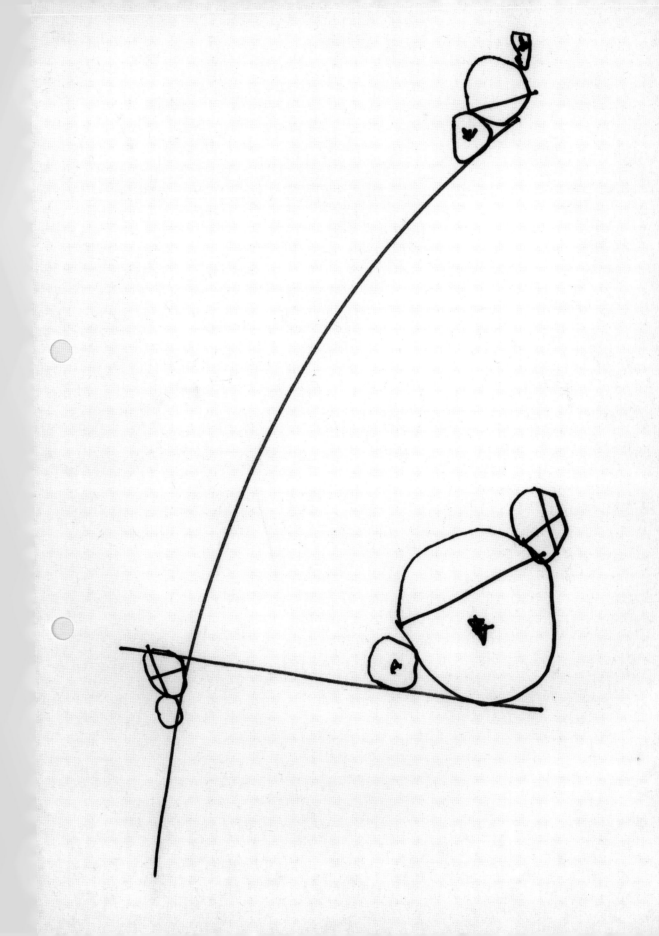

"Whats his angle then 'cos I don't get where he's coming from."

"The mans not interested in that.... Measure the arm, have you got a reach? Shoulder to shoulder to knuckle. He never had it, no no reach but always a mouthful of words

One day he wrote it down and people said thats never gonna work. The man 'jus let go of his consciousness,

let it [...]
Kinda really [...]
like [...]
someone [...]
him - you [...]
it takes [...]
of a sudden

Yeah, settin it to music, makin tunes.... no 'em, no,' jus cooing like a baby all over 'em. treat. Now he's famous, people read all kinds into it. Almost come to nothing, almost obscurity, almost.... Damn, he's so on top [...] can get near it. He's got famous without meaning it." "Then !!" "Then what !

The road of a drifter

le,

ve,

out,
mad
lios

lo

but
ll
roll...

ing
d a

shit
ed into

e

You wanna understand this ... or
taste it ... you've gotta live it, you know.
Then it's personal. That comes from you,
who you grew up with.
It goes without saying. You, me, the
our own frame, set it up and lea
That's what something means.

...you've gotta feel it,
experience it.
background, where you grew up,
... we're always gonna bring
it that way. --

What something means.

"Yeah" she says, really slowly... "Idea ... Idea...
A.O.L.O.G.Y..... don't make me laugh."

smiles "I'm not interested in your
...aganda, all that propaganda. Today.
...ore, after. beyond. I'm ~~between~~
... You wanna give it a name
...gullable, but me, I'm not that.
... know I'm fabulous, and that's
...remember. Glamour, whatever

... be."

... you've got choices" I say,

...:

...ked and she did look good.

...ou got a better Idea."

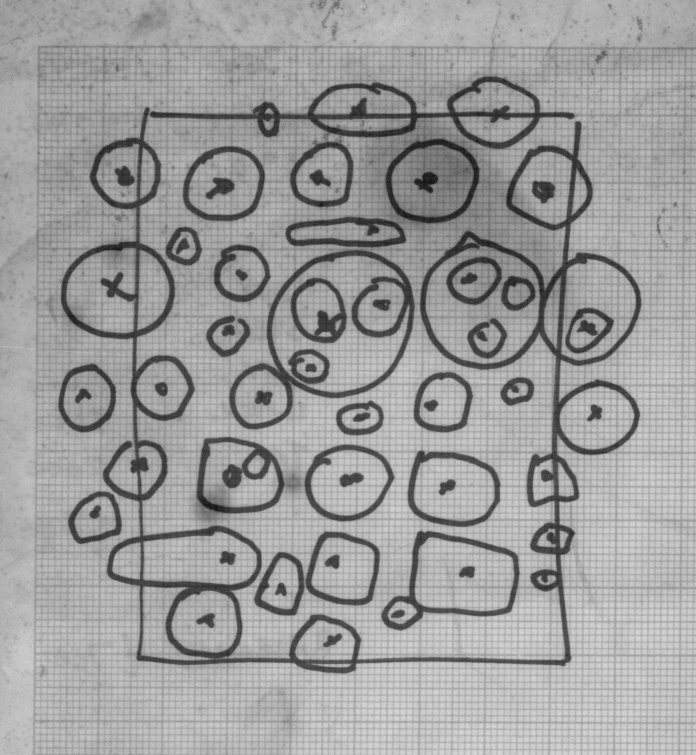

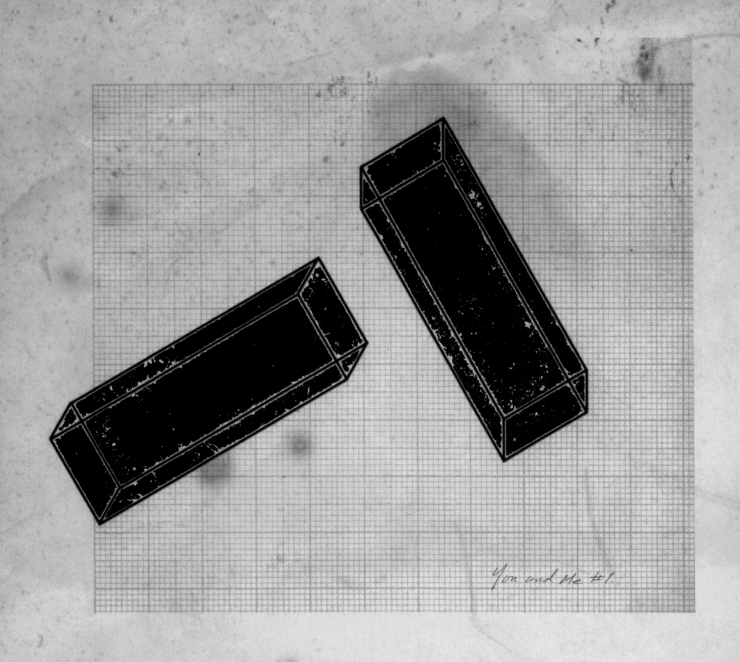

You and Me #1.

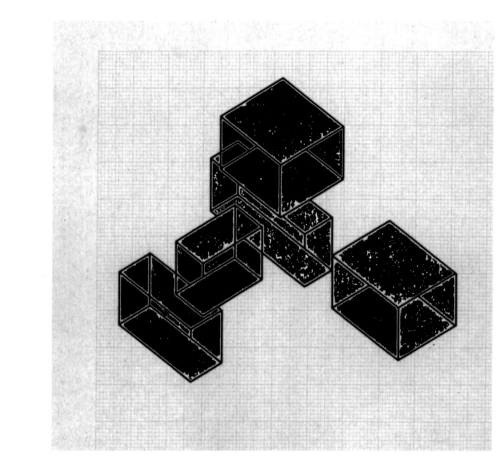

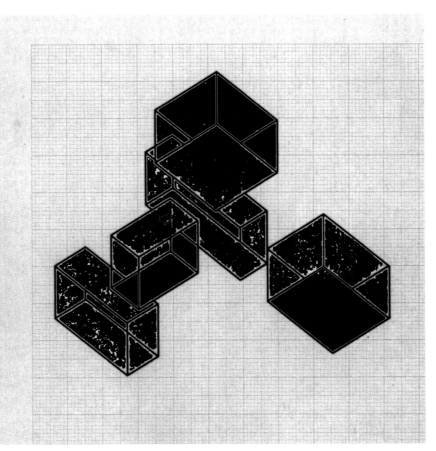

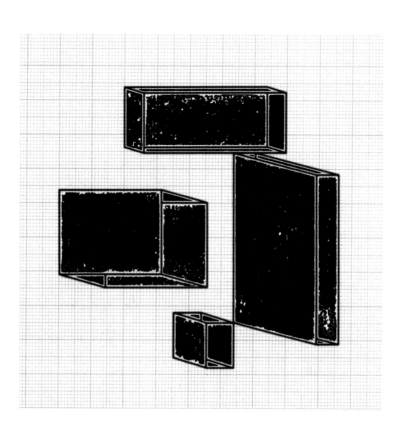

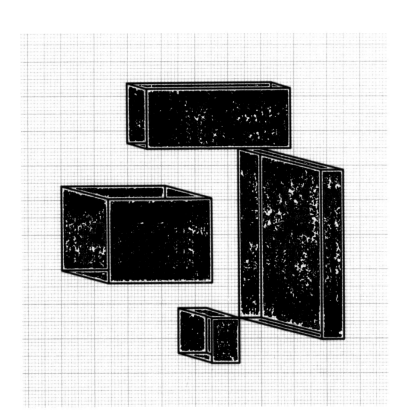

The Girl Thing

The story of two working class slovenly ⌐
cycle that never ends. It's a story of brava⌐
respect must be shown to old people ladies ⌐
an obsessive regard for clean washing.

The two men drive their Mercedes 280CE!
a laundrette incongruously set within a bar
and re-wash a pile of brilliant white linen
talks incessantly recounting the intimate deta⌐
recent past. Is this perhaps a way of him dea⌐
circumstances? His long suffering friend listen⌐
aware of their predicament and the necessity

As the tale unfolds against the backdrop of their
involved in a car crash, a romantic and a la⌐

d in a loop as
t in a world where
dogs, coupled with
from and back to
ndscape to search
One of the characters
or event from his
th his own
parents seeming more
volve out of it.
we become
guide to fancy shoes.

Dead Heat.

Sittin' here watchin' it... I haven't got a clue what's really going on &
there's something keeping me here, glued to it, like nothin' else matters....

A, B, C, D and E set off on track, trotting, building fast up to a jog, 'til th'
reach a steady rhythm just inside a sprint. F, G, H all the way through to Z
and beyond, they're in tow, jostling for pace, a position, but only A to E
really feature. They're the faces I recognise, they're the ones I count on. "A"
looks good out in front, B and C have got potential. I'm beginning to recognise the
faces more than D and E. A and B push hard, get ahead, leaving C to fall
back two steps as the rhythm finds a new pattern. I've placed my bet. A still
neck and neck with B. I've recognised that face over the other. A's the man.
"A". He breaks pace, moves forward, regains pace. I concentrate on his face
alone, I can't read the insignia, the colours are all muddied grey. I
recognise A only by physical characteristics, skin tone, age...

I'm distracted... I look away, then...

Back... but the leader, the front runner, his face has changed... it's not
the face of A, or B. I think back to C but it's not C either. C was tall
thin. The new face... he's out of nowhere. "A" was black. The new A is
white... I don't get it, I can't tell you why, then I see, it's all different
now. It's all changed. A baton race, a relay marathon. The new leader, A2,
he's taken over from A1. I'm forced to recognise a new leader, my team, my
winner, out in front. This face is the one.... Or did B1 change baton before
A1 giving B2 the lead. I'm uncertain... I was distracted. The face in front is
probably A2 but possibly B2... I have to settle on the combination A/B2.
I watch A/B2 make a push forward, the pace is good, the distance from
the pack increases. A/B2 is a good 7, 10 paces ahead of B/C2. Here it
comes, the second baton change, a new runner, a new face to study, to

memorise. A/B3, it's all I've got to go on. The track suits a different tone of grey, the team has no standard, no number on the runners, no mark that defines the group, only an alphabet I can't read pinned on the team shirt, to me indistinguishable from all other team shirts.

Commercial break.... the T.V. shows me something I don't want.... Stop. We're back on track, I watch a set of new faces sprint towards me. I'm lost once more, I don't recognise them, only my combination. The front runner becomes A/B/C 4 leading B/C/A 4 from C/B/A 4. Then disaster, B/C/A 4 trips, stumbles, bringing down A/B/C 4 into a bloody crumpled mess on the tarmac, leaving C/B/A 4 to take the lead. A/B/C 4 won't give up. Nor B/C/A 4, it's their race, they must continue, find the pace ....
... catch C/B/A 4. Now it's neck and neck between all three. The gap is closing, the finish line approaching. There's still time, once more, a last burst of energy.

The T.V. shows me slow motion images.

The frames jog through their cycle. Runners look like agonized puppets moving through a clearly defined cycle played out in fragile frozen moments, each a replicant of the other. This I realise is all that counts. The single cycle. Left foot down, right foot forward and down followed by left foot forward. The whole race has been that cycle .... just once. I watch C/B/A 4, A/B/C 4 and B/C/A 4 come in together in a dead heat.

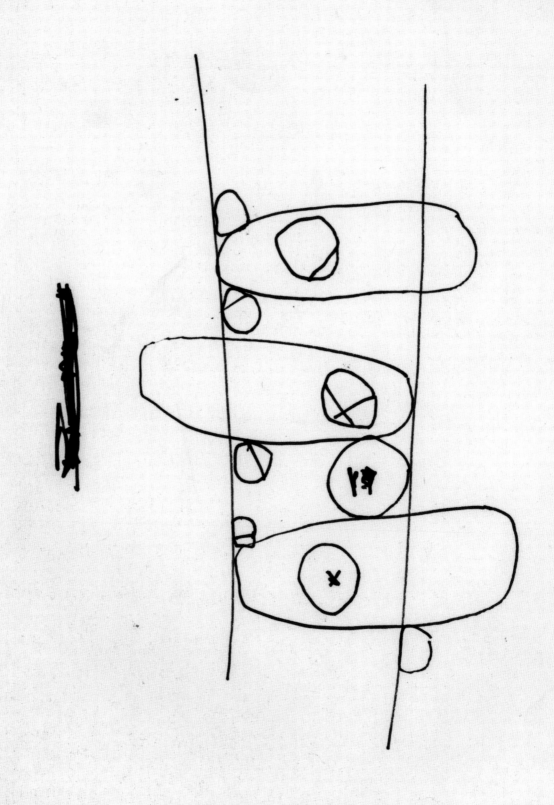

The Two Men

Charlie's watching Harry,
He doesn't trust him.
Harry knows it, pays no attention
Charlie keeps watching.

The two men will laugh about everything.
The two men will laugh about nothing.
The two men will harm one another.
The two men will become each other.
The two men ....

The whole point is...

The whole point of this is to be as obvious as possible.
A is A. B is B. We go between. Left, right, don't look sideways. Toe
the line, it's how we want you to be.
Totally fuckin boring.... Fuck that.
They pretend. We pretend!
I wanna eat more cornflakes, the ones with the sugar coated crunch,
the ones that'll make me fit, healthy and rich. Yeah... the ones that
give me all that free time.
Freedom with sugar coated cornflakes. Does this suit me?
Yeah it looks great on you. You look like one of the signs I'll follow all
my life, all my life till my eyes won't focus any more... Fuck that.

The whole point is to be as obvious as possible.
A is still A, B is still B, we still go between. Faster this time, never
slower. We become a danger when we slow down. Slow is bad but
fast is... faster. Fast is good but slow is good when its fast to be
slow. I'll be told in good time.

The whole point of this is to be as obvious as possible. A and B haven't changed...

Are we sure we're still representing A as he / she would really feel comfortable?

Well I don't know, whadda you think?

I think fast but this is slow... good slow or bad slow? Two questions now, another one and will have enough points to make a straight line, one that starts with A but moves off with its' own direction and speed. An event within, outside the obvious.

But the whole point of this is to be as obvious as possible.

Whadda you think?

I thought. You wait. I'll tell. You'll say "I don't understand." You've forgotten, I've remembered.

Three points make a straight line but...

We only need one point.

Is A still recognizable as A because we have to get to B as fast as possible... There must be no confusion about that. A to B. Not whats between, only whats at the end.

Fuck that...

90% of it

...drunk, we know that. We know exactly what he's like, what he wants. And there's no confusion from the character working the door either. A proffesional. Paid up to stand up, has a sixth sense, this is business not pleasure. A work situation.

"I was put down" says the boy.

"I'm not even gonna look at you" sparks the pro.

There's no answer good enough, the heavy doesn't even glance at the list, 'jus stands there looking... Leavy. The boy focuses hard and makes a run for it, double vision. There's the crowd, the bright lights, the gap, just wide enough.... and then he's in, down the stairs, past the coats, in the thick.

And you know what, pissed or not. once you're in, well thats 90% of it.

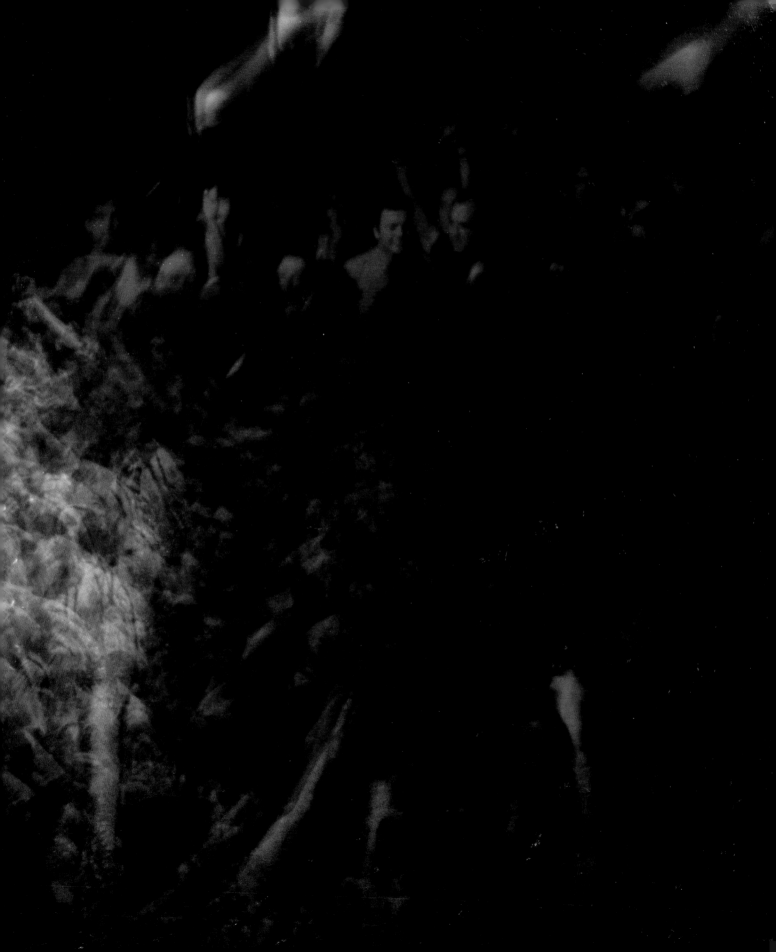

" "

how can I know what I think till I see what I say?

alice

" "

why is this work resonant? what is it about 'our place in the world' that the work enacts; re-enacts?

mark pimlott. carl andre: more like roads than like buildings. carl andre and the sculptural imagination. museum of modern art oxford. edited ian cole. 1996. p44-45.

" "

(a) confirmation of the world as it appears to me •

jean paul sartre, war diaries: notebook from a phoney war 1939-40, verso,1984. p129.

" "

continuous project altered daily •

robert morris. continuous project altered daily, the writings of robert morris. mit. 1995.

"

repeating then is in every one, in every one their being and their feeling and their way of realizing everything and everyone comes out of them in repeating...slowly every one in continuous repeating, to their minutest variation, comes to be clearer

"

to some one •

gertrude stein. the gradual making of the making of americans. the selected writings of gertrude stein. vintage books, 1990. p258.

"

i think the artist is one that takes 'a vow of conversation...'
(...an exploration of silences and meanings with which my consciousness never manages to be quite simultaneous but in which my body is

"

always present) •

thomas merton, quoted in negotiating rapture, the power of art to transform lives. introduction, richard francis. museum of contemporary art, chicago.1996. p6.

"

drawing is the first visible form in my works...the first visible thing of the form of the thought, the changing point from the invisible powers to the visible thing...

"

everything now comes together • • •

joseph beuys, thinking is form, thames and hudson, 1993, p73.

" "

the world is all that is the case •

ludwig wittgenstein, tractatus logico-philosphicus, translated by d.f. prears and b.f.mcguiness. routledge and kegan paul. 1961.

" "

what travels through me is what i make •

tracey emin, frieze 34, 1997, p56.

still point: turning world

" "

a still point in the turning world

t.s. eliot

process; a tomato project

this essay follows on from the previous text in   . it revisits, continues and expands the concerns and issues of my life.

on drawing. for as long as i can remember i have had compulsion to draw, to make marks with whatever material was at hand. from the very beginning the why, what, how, where, developed an engagement with the process of looking and the mechanics of materiality within the context of the world. inthisworldtogether.

one of my favourite walks with my grandfather was to the ancient sussex village of wilmington. carved into the chalk hill, high above the churchyard, was a large prehistoric figure, some 200' high. for a seven year old it was a place of magic and wonder that fuelled my interest in drawing. i loved the idea that there was continuity in the process of mark making, it rooted the experience of drawing in the process of time.

was drawing with the material of the hill and that material was somehow transmuted by the process of drawing into an image. the image had a reality of its own within the context of the world and i was the conduit between the image and the world.

" ...precipitation from the sea accumulated in the clouds and was deposited on land as rain which filtered through the soil to the river to rejoin the sea once more. not only did this express interconnectivity, evolution and journey, it also meant that the same object could have "

different relationships and functions •
process; a tomato project. thames and hudson, 1996.

" we are not ᶦⁿ the world, we become ʷⁱᵗʰ the world "
deleuze and guattari, gilles deleuze, essays critical and clinical, verso, 1998, pxxxiv

" the process of change seems to be continuous, and continuity seems to be the primary context of infinity. the continuous is "

what is infinitely divisible •
aristotle, the physics, book III, 200b16.

" in all space each thing and each human being is at the center... each one... is the most honored one of all. interpenetration (with and)... by every other one... each and everything...is related to each and every other thing. interpenetration means that each one of these most honored ones of all... moving out in all directions penetrating and being penetrated by every other one, no matter what time or what the space. so that when one says that there is no cause and effect, what is meant is that there are incalculable infinity of causes and effects, that in fact each and every thing, in all time and space, is related to each and every other thing in all of time and space. this being so there is no need to cautiously proceed in dualistic terms of success and failure or the beautiful and the ugly or good and evil, but rather simply to walk on "

'not wondering' •
silence, john cage. wesleyan university press. 1973. p46-47

" ...there is no neutral site. every context has its frame and its ideological overtones. "

it's a matter of degree
richard serra , sculpture, moma ny, 1986. p49

" should we believe the photograph represents the 'objective truth' while the painting records the artist's subjective vision – the way he transformed 'what he saw'?...take the image on the artist's retina. it sounds scientific enough, but actually there never was one such image "

which we could single out for comparison with either photograph or painting •
professor ernst gombrich in 'truth and the stereotype', the essential gombrich, phaidon, 1996, p91
(referring to cézanne's paintings of mont saint-victoire and photographs of the mountain taken from the same vantage point)

" an endless whole, a wave without horizon, without shore •
claude monet. quoted in vija clemins, work 1964-1996, edited by james lingwood, institute of contemporary arts, 1996. p27 "

" the edge of the sea concerned with "

itself
william carlos williams, excerpt from 'landscape with the fall of icarus', william carlos williams selected poems, new direction books, 1985, p238

" the tao that cannot be told is not the eternal tao.
the name that can be named is not the eternal name.
the nameless is the beginning of heaven and earth.
the named is the mother of ten thousand things.
even desireless, one can see the mystery.
even desiring, one can see the manifestations.
these two spring from the same source but differ in name;
this appears as darkness.
darkness within darkness. "

the gate to all mystery •
lao tsu tao te ching. one. translated by gia-fu feng and jane english. vintage, 1972, p3

" (...an exploration of silences and meanings with which my consciousness never manage

to be quite simultaneous but in which my body is always present) "
thomas merton, quoted in negotiating rapture, the power of art to transform lives. introduction, richard francis. museum of contemporary art, chicago. 1996. p6

on one of those walks my grandfather pointed to the sea and asked me where i thought the shoreline was. from our vantage point high on the cliffs the line seemed discernible enough, but as we walked towards it the relationship between the shore and the sea became problematic. to add to an already confusing situation my grandfather added that if we took a millimetre rule, a centimetre rule and a metre rule we could then measure the shore but we would get very different results. the smaller the calibre of measurement the longer the shore would be. as we continued walking down the steep incline to the sea the shoreline became more complex. he added: if we could just stop time would we include those pebbles that were still wet but not touched by the sea or only those that were immersed? how did we know what pebbles were still wet? the naked eye and a specialist instrument might give you very different, even contradictory, results. and what if it was raining?

my grandfather then asked me about the relationship [edgelessness] between the dirt track that we had just left and the area of grass surrounding it and about the clouds floating within the sky above. where were the edges? where did one thing stop and another start? i remember feeling that the world was a far less certain place than i once thought.

" cage drew the inspiration for 4'33"...from the series of 'white' paintings by his friend and sometime colleague robert rauschenberg. as rauschenberg postulated the dynamic of his paintings as their reaction to the changing light in the rooms which they might be hung, and the conditions created coming and going in those rooms, so cage conceived 4'33", as a piece of music constantly in flux, subject to the ambient sounds surrounding each performance.

american pioneers: ives to cage and beyond. chapter 5, john cage. alan rich. phaidon press, 1995. p.142

" and since silence is fundamentally auratic in its manifestation – as benjamin writes with reference of baudelaire – modern or even post-modern man, the man of 'mechanical reproducibility', is obliged, in the midst of the noisy labyrinth of meditations, information and reproductions, sometimes to impose silence and submit to the uncanniness of what "

comes back ● ● ●

" a thinking of an origin that has nothing to do with a nostalgia for the past, but that concerns precisely the productive collision between the now and an unexpected, "

re-invented then ●

" if in (cage's) onement I newman breaks definitely with any objectified depth of space, he reconnects, it seems to "

me, 'with the physical sensation' of a depth of place ●

[in reference to onement I]

" ...as benjamin says 'however close an apparition', a distance suddenly irrupts within it. it irrupts here in the reverse, in the retrait contrived (and not drawn, outlined or situated) by newman. in that sense, it places us squarely before a kind of dialectic of place – close/distant, in front of/inside, tactile/optical, appearing/disappearing, open/closed, hollowed out/saturated – which confers on the image its most fundamental auratic quality. it is an inchoate rhythm of black and white, a 'physical "

sensation of time' ● ● ●

georges didi-huberman, the supposition of the aura: the now, the then, and modernity. negotiating rapture. museum of contemporary art, chicago. 1996, p49/61.

" an uncarved block is wiser than another block carved with the prince's law: in that the assertion of one law obliterates all others while the uncarved block retains the wisdom of "

all laws ●

carl andre, quoted in: carl andre and the sculptural imagination. museum of modern art oxford. edited ian cole. 1996, p33

" all at once/straight off I smeared the map of everyday "

vladimir mayakovsky. but could you?-a cubist still life. missal of three. 1913. juliette r. stapanian, reproduced in mayakovsky's cubo-futurist vision, rice university press, 1986, p58

in and out of sight
in and out of touch
in and out of mind
in and out of love
in and out of breath
in and out of line
in and out of bounds
in and out of space
in and out of time
in and out of
in   out
  and   of

" that any colour | that anywhere | that anything
be anywhere | be anything | be any colour
for anything | for any colour | for anywhere "

jasper johns, writings, sketchbook notes, interviews, the museum of modern art, new york, 1996, p71 in my subsequent attempts to draw i could not disassociate myself from the obvious questions; 'what am i drawing?' and 'who am i?'. the symbiotic relationship between the drawing itself and the condition of drawing was, to me, a material fact. moreover it seemed to have a direct relationship to the issues of the self in the world.

it also placed the act of drawing within a conceptual and cultural complex. it was not only the most direct form of expression in order to quantify my experience but it also transformed looking into seeing, and seeing was process. the work that resulted from this process is the map of my journey.

the map is inconclusive
since neither the internal nor external are static.
the map is inconclusive
since neither the form nor content are static.
the map is inconclusive
since neither the search nor journey are static.
the map is inconclusive
since neither the individual spirit nor the world are static.

" negotiation strives towards an 'equalization through a common denominator' (derrida). if rapture is sublime seizure, a caesura in everyday life, negotiation (neg [not] – otium [ease, quiet]) emanates from "

noise, the unquiet of the day's business ●

" aligning negotiation with the system of social exchange – language, action, signification, representation at the centre of contemporary life, at the cusp of the creation of commodities and the initiation of communication. concerned primarily with the disclosure of the human subject as agent, negotiation is the ability to articulate differences in space and time, to link words and images in new symbolic orders, to intervene in the forest of signs and mediate what may seem to be "

incommensurable values or contradictory realities ●
homi k. bhabha, aura and agora, on negotiating rapture and speaking between, negotiating rapture, museum of contemporary art, chicago, 1996, p8

" methodstructureintentiondisciplinenotationindeterminancyinterpenetrationdevotioncircumstancesvariablestructurenotunderstandingcontingencyinconsistencyperform
title of cage's 1988 norton lecture at harvard quoted in; american pioneers: ives to cage and beyond. chapter 5, john cage. alan rich. phaidon press, 1995. p.180

in 1961 cage defined his intention as;

" ● ● ● to affirm this life, not bring order out of chaos... but simply to wake up to the very life we're living, which is "

so excellent once one lets it...act of its own accord ●
quoted in; american pioneers: ives to cage and beyond. chapter 5, john cage. alan rich. phaidon press, 1995. p.165

" the communication process goes on in order to achieve some sort of shared reality. this stands on marked opposition to a theory of indoctrination which has associations to submission, compliance, "

and lack of participation ●
richard francis, negotiating rapture, an introduction, negotiating rapture, museum of contemporary art, chicago, 1996, p5

" the best service, the bravest, is to stop designing, in the "

ways we do now, and to try for something better ●
john chris jones, designing designing, adt 1991. p80

" instead of copying a territory, the map creates a new reality which is another map, a ma so concrete (territory-map) or so abstract (map-territory) that it cancels itself as such and suggests another map, a map to the second degree, itself referring to a third, and so on "

until infinity ●
gilles a. tiberghien, land art, art data, 1993, p171

" i was to move from structure to process, from music as an object having parts to music "

without beginning, middle or end, music as weather ●
john cage, 1952 quoted in; american pioneers: ives to cage and beyond. chapter 5, john cage. alan rich. phaidon press, 1995. p.163

" i want to stress two aspects that are always present in my work and which I feel should contained in all human action: both the solemnity of the self-determination of one's own life a "

one's own gestures as well as the modesty of our own actions at all times ●
joseph beuys im gespräch mit michele bonuomo. dec 1985. in beuys zu ehren, ed. by arman zweite, munich, 1986, p93.

" " at every point in nature there is something to see
jasper johns, writings, sketchbook notes, interviews, the museum of modern art, new york, 1996

" from above it is not bright;
from below it is not dark:
an unbroken thread beyond description.
it returns to nothingness.
the form of the formless,
the image of the imageless,
it is called indefinable and beyond imagination.

stand before it and there is no beginning.
follow it and there is no end.
stay with the ancient tao, "

move with the present ●
lao tsu, tao te ching, fourteen. translated by gia-fu feng and jane english. vintage, 1972, p30-31

" for the listener, who listens in the snow,
and, nothing himself, beholds "

nothing that is not there and nothing that is
wallace stevens, excerpt from the snow man. the palm at the end of the mind. vintage, 1972. p54

he map might also be a map referring to the process
of creation of the map's connection with the world. by
means of its construction the map bears evidence of
the process of thought and both physical presence and
physical action.
he map is therefore the physical evidence of the process
of negotiation and the production of this map is governed
by the interplay of my senses, memories and dreams
and through the process of personal navigation the map
s continually redrawn, the process of process.

n my grandfather's analogies the objects themselves
become signs in order to express an abstract.

where is the edge of a cloud?
where is the edge of a thought?
where is the edge of the spoken word?

what had seemed to me to be a concrete form of
description and communication suddenly became
unstable and open to interpretation and expression. in
this process of analogy and metaphor what is concrete?
when concrete and certainty are obviously relative terms.
t was obvious that there were always alternative ways
of expressing a similar condition but never the same
condition; because same does not truly exist.

for the past 20 years i've struggled to draw. what was a 'continuous process altered daily' came to a halt when the thin line between having facility and being facile was all too obviously breached.

the only time that I ever took pencil to paper was when i drew the sea. for some reason the nature of the subject (the sea), the object (the drawing) and the process (the act of drawing – conceptually and aesthetically) made intuitive sense.

this january, while holidaying in tasmania, i decided to draw the landscape again. after the first few attempts there wasn't the sense of failure that i had been experiencing. something else was happening. by the time i arrived in adelaide i couldn't wait to start again.

i realised that my reading of space had been culturally conditioned. i wasn't seeing but merely looking, contriving to fit the world in front of me into what i 'knew' to be the established order of space. this perspectival conditioning was so insidious that i was unconsciously wrapping the image of what i was looking at over the 'model' and then convincing myself that that is what i saw.

when i sat down in front of a mass of trees i tried to empty myself of the 'model' and draw what i actually saw, the field of vision as one entity. the sustained process of drawing became one moment.

for five hours i immersed myself in the complexities of the scene in front of me. darker areas, such as the shadows beneath the closest trees receded, whereas the lighter areas, such as the sunlit tips of the trees that were further back, projected. space turned, twisted and inverted itself before my eyes. the conventional reading was only evident in the immediate surroundings. the space beyond that, about 20 metres away, became 'field'- either a psycho-geography of a metaphysical topology or a flat perpendicular plane. this wasn't a 'cubist' reading, an intellectual analysis and reconstruction to reveal the (reality of) objectivity of known masses, but a complex surface that simultaneously confirmed and denied its spatial form within its own, everchanging reality.

the drawing explains itself. the surface of the drawing was entirely flat, complex matrices of tiny marks describing the 'space'. these marks held their own 'reality' which was quite different to any of my previous drawings.

the immediate foreground seemed to obey conventional reading, elsewhere the forms leapt in and out of the drawn space. the relationships between adjacent areas altered accordingly. what appeared recessive in one area became projective when read in the context of other areas, and by doing so denied the 'rules' of the perspectival model.

this is what i saw not what i thought i should see. the world explains itself.

,1,18

17,19,

,9,...

like my grandfather my father worked with numbers all his life. where my grandfather shaped values in alphanumeric expressions and saw poetry and transience in the world my father was more a numerical engineer taking little notice of context or philosophy. in his work things added up, there were no ambivalences, no areas of negotiation or transience, just the self-regulating momentum of the method and a sum finished. there were no discursive walks, i can't even remember having a philosophical conversation with him, but he had the calm centre of a craftsman at peace with both himself and his life. for me that very stillness was what made him special.

his death, however, was traumatic and violent. a series of heart attacks and strokes dismantled both his self and his reason. words, thoughts, sentences became a contortion of expression mirrored by the tremendous physical pain that inflicted both his mind and body. after two years the convulsions finally put paid to any coherent word or thought.

after a particularly harrowing day i returned to sit quietly by his bedside, just holding his hand and watching him sleep. after an hour or so he stirred, breathing irregularly he began to utter sounds and then numbers. fast, short, dense bursts were followed by long silences, occasionally punctuated by a single digit.

slowly the numbers became less distinct. each inhalation abstracted whatever he was trying to say. the sounds themselves became less formed as they became abstracted tones until they became barely audible.

after a while his lips finally closed

I'm standing in the desert under the old light of long-dead stars. There is a warm, gentle wind blowing through the night. I have just walked out of Shoshone to where the road meets the desert. There, the hard edge of tarmac gives way to soft sand and sage brush and it's not long before you can begin to forget that there was a road back there in the first place. I've walked out here from Shoshone, the place we aimed for on the map some two days ago. Back in Shoshone earlier that night, in a little former-Indian trading post, we drank MGD from thick, icy beer glasses in a pizza parlour that doubled as a bar and a pool hall. Across the blacktop road stood the motel where we'd got ourselves a room for the night. On taking the key from the proprietess around midday we were told that the second key on the ring gave us access to the swimming pool: in the middle of the desert this idea came as something of a surprise. But, later that afternoon we walked up a dirt track, past several little bungalows and shacks, each with an emerald green square of lawn outside its front door, each defying the desert and maintaining the frontier, to a place up in the rocks where we found a big, blue-watered swimming pool. Fed by springs from the mountains, the pool was fenced off with steel chicken wire from wild animals and those who had not paid their dues to the Shoshone Water Sports Club. The incongruity of the pool in the desert rockscape was emphasised by the lack of people making use of it in the heat of the early afternoon. That day, under the blue sky only two of Shoshone's inhabi-

tants were taking the waters. The couple, a man and a woman, were well matched. He: a big old guy, grey haired and swimming slowly up and down, she: wearing a hat and sunglasses sitting on a sun lounger and reading a pulp novel with a gold-blocked cover. He was the garrulous one. His first words to us were "Where are you from?" I answered: "London". "Come to see how the poor people live?" was his somewhat unwelcoming and gruff reply. We made a little small talk after that, while his wife continued to read, not having spoken a word. She was probably used to his bluff manner and the way he liked to strike up confrontational conversations with the strangers who drifted into Shoshone. We spent the afternoon splashing and swimming in the pool and reading on the hot wooden deck that surrounded the water, and then we went back to the motel where we lay on the bed and listened to the air conditioning whirring and vibrating on its fixture in the window frame. I watched some silent TV. The room smelt slightly stale; of cigarettes and cleaning agents. The sound of the air conditioning, the flickering anonymity of the television pictures and the stillness of the desert outside made me think of all the other people who had stayed here in the middle of the desert, in this room, over the years. I think we probably held each other a little and then drifted in and out of sleep until it was time to go and eat and have some drinks with the locals over in Shoshone's only nightspot, the bar and pizzeria. The atmosphere in that place, with its dark wood bar

WHICH DO NOT PERTAIN TO THE STORY AT HAND. IF WE PRESENT PERSONAL HISTORY AS FICTION, HOWEVER, THE FICTION MAY HAVE THE POSSIBILITY OF CONTAINING MANY TRUTHS.

and gingham table cloths was friendly enough. There were maybe five customers in there when we arrived and as many people working the kitchens, bussing and tending bar. The room was long and roughly divided into a dining area and the bar. We sat on stools near the front of the room. The storefront window that looked out onto the road was dominated by a big Miller sign in yellow and white neon which made it difficult to see outside into the gathering darkness. We drank our beers and chatted with the women who worked there and we told them a little about where we were from and then we shot some pool together. Country music played softly in the background as the evening progressed through a kind of mutual curiosity defined as much by our foreignness to each other as by the banter between us and the Americans. At one point in the evening all of us in the bar stopped and watched as a big Peterbilt tractor was dragged through Shoshone's only street by an even bigger breakdown truck. The huge and once powerful machine being towed was kind of bent and broken: in this place where you sensed that little of any real drama ever happened, the wreck was a dramatic sight, moving slowly through the little town drawing stares in its wake. In the bar, the serving girls made their way to the window and looked with us through the yellow glare of the beer advertisement. "Lord God," said one of them, "I sure hope that no-one was hurt in that." She spoke in a soft American accent and shook her head as she thought about the moment of impact or the guy's family or whatever. After we had watched the slow pageant of crumpled heavy machinery pass the windows the atmosphere in the bar was a little more reflective, a little more subdued than it had been, as if everyone there had had something foretold for them. The surety of American machinery, American steel, at once curiously real and curiously hollow, had been revealed momentarily as something potentially lesser than it looked to be. For a moment the pounding beat of America's ceaseless travelling, the ecstasy of its communications with itself, had ceased. Such a big place with so many people, but solipsistically so, tends to be immured against the idea of failure. Even so, America gets little intimations of its potential for dissolution in moments such as these.

America is a nation at peace with itself until some clue to the fallibility of its modern tools, if not its people, hoves into view. Aircrashes, the Challenger disaster, the last big Californian 'quake, the failure of the US automotive industry, the grinding, underfunded railways, these things seem to highlight the fallibility of the culture's – in truth any culture's – reliance on technology for its sense of reality, legitimacy and authenticity. But these qualities are not all that America offers its citizens, this cheap technology and freedom, of course they aren't. Out there in the desert those tiny green lawns staked out on the sandy floor are a vestigial trace of the real frontier spirit: watered and tended and fenced with miniature picket and studded with posies in the summer, they are signs of the human capacity to care about the marks we leave and the signs we make on the earth for others to read. These marks are important. These are the gardens of Eden, as far as America is concerned, where in general, the fall has yet to come. This, in part, is what America gives Americans: a chance, often literally, to make something of themselves and by extension, to make something of their surroundings. When faced with a desert, that sense of opportunity and the need to survive must be exponentially increased, hence, I guess, something like the Shoshone Water Sports Club springs into existence. The lawns and the Water Sports Club in Shoshone are evidence of humanity striving to subsist in an inhuman environment. The pizza they served in the little bar was good

and the chillies on it cut with the cold beer in a perfect way. Having drunk another beer we told the bar that we were on our way to Las Vegas. The people in the bar were just a little short of incredulous at this news. "We never go there," said one dark-haired woman." If we want to get a Vegas experience or to gamble or to live it up we just go over the hill to Parumph." I said I thought that Parumph sounded interesting but that Vegas was somehow more attractive just by dint of its fame. It was the kind of thing, I explained, that if you were English, would lure you there for the spectacle, even if it was just the once. They all said the same was true of Parumph, but understood the lure of Vegas to those travelling across the desert and agreed that we should see the place, spend some

money and then get the hell out of there. Parumph paled into the background as an option — these guys just weren't selling it hard enough. It was after this conversation about where to go, the pluses and minuses of places, that I took the little walk along the road into the quiet of the desert and began to look up, or rather, down at the stars. There was an eerie quiet in the countryside underlined by the wind moving through the sage and the sound of small animals baying and yelping in the distance. Far enough away from the few street lamps it seemed to get darker around my eyes and the stars sprang into relief against the night sky. I lay down on the earth only marginally mindful that there might be snakes or other predators slithering around or looking for a meal. These thoughts of threat from other earth dwellers vanished as I began to perceive what I was looking at as I lay there on the warm dusty earth. The old light of long dead stars, young stars and galaxies shone down on me. I could see space a great deal more clearly than I had seen it before anywhere else on the earth, the detail of the composition, the infinite variety of organisation which made the universe what it is. I could see out of the corner of my eye what I thought to be dust clouds or other smaller galaxies and I swear that some of them were spiral in form. But whenever I tried to look directly at them, to fix them with my minuscule eye and my own tiny human lens, I could not see them. These entities were only visible if I did not look straight at them. As I lay there, I also saw many tiny shooting stars: pieces of debris that had travelled from God knows where to flare briefly in the friction of our thick, gravity-held atmosphere. As I looked up at the silver specks and blobs in the night sky, there were some recognisable constellations and many more unseen by my eyes, I saw space as a place full of other places. I could clearly make out the shape of the edge of our own place, our milky way, itself composed of many other stars and systems and galaxies beyond. There on the desert sand I was amazed by what I could see with just my eyes. The immensity of it and the way these clumps of light and matter were arranged haphazardly through space and time, flung outwards and still travelling that way, away, away. Some years later, I was reminded of lying on the desert floor and looking at the stars as I flew back into London's Heathrow Airport from Stockholm. Delays had meant that the plane had been rerouted to come in over Scotland and then fly down the centre of England. It was winter and the night was early dark. On the ground from some 37,000 feet up, England was black and the only distinguishable features were the agglomerations of sodium light that defined cities and major trunk roads. England was etched in sodium light. From that altitude in the crystalline dark night air, the gold of the sodium shone brilliantly and town upon town was visible into the distance, seemingly joined by traces of golden thread. These were tiny roads, as fine as filaments of communication. As we flew the length of the country and I drank in the sight, I tried to imagine this vista layered upon itself so that there were now several layers of cities and towns seen from 37,000 feet. Were our cities not tied to the earth, we'd be able to replicate the positions in space of galaxies to one another in the shape of our cities, and ideas like north and south, up and down, here and there would have a little less meaning as a result. We travelled to Las Vegas in the early morning of the next day, catching a big breakfast from the Denny's restaurant on the way and pushing on so that we made Excalibur well before nightfall. Excalibur is an extraordinary thing. A castle which is not a castle, an architectural idea plundered from Europe as if Europe were one big country in which all the signs of culture co-exist at the same time, all the time. Thus this Hotel has mansard roofs and lancet windows, French chateau styling and a fake drawbridge. Excalibur plays with Arthurian legends and houses a casino, sleeps a couple of thousand, I should think, and when it was built it was the biggest hotel anywhere in the world. Once inside, the poor American staff who are asked to wear wimples and tabards, hose and doublets are unfailingly polite in the way that Americans are when they are serving you, yet in spite of the enforced olde worlde charm, no transactions can take place as a guest of the hotel without a credit card imprint. Without the means to replace money, to gain credit, as far as Excalibur is concerned, you simply are not allowed to exist in its world: this is a little strange in a place that is built on the ownership of money,

and on the exchange of money on games of chance. What has been constructed here in Las Vegas, with the absence of money, the presence of the idea of money, the fake history and the people – is a little world of unauthentic effect. Unlike the experience in the bar in Shoshone where the good values that grow between humans seemed to hold sway – conversation, care, a sense of place, community and survival, the Las Vegas experience was almost entirely the opposite. Las Vegas is based on the anonymous consumption of the hyperreal, the desert on the other hand offers the potential for the personal communion with the sidereal. Unlike Shoshone, Las Vegas is all commodity exchange: from the blank-eyed parade of topless dancers to the newspapers offering "room service",

from the guy who followed us for a block along the strip in the hot night, his hood up, his sneakers quiet on the pavement (we escaped up the drawbridge of Excalibur, our fake castle and sanctuary), to the cabs, the food bars and the other hotels: New York, the Pirate one, the MGM one and the Egyptian one, the smaller casinos and show houses, it's all there in exchange for the dollar. Although the exchange usually takes place based on the idea of the dollar and not the dollar itself – the credit card keeps the wheels of commerce oiled and rolling. It's a funny thing when the symbols of value and exchange are replaced by yet other symbols, like the tokens that are used instead of dollars in the casinos. It's rather like putting a handle on the toilet seat for the purposes of hygiene. The logical extension of course is to attach a handle to the handle ad infinitum, to create greater and greater layers of distance between the original source of potential infection and ourselves. As we would with such a mad lavatory seat handle, we as a culture are trying to sanitise our relationship with money. I can't say that I blame us for doing so. Money stinks, it really does. When it's new it smells of inks and chemicals, of bleaching agents, paper and washdowns, but when it's old, when it has lived and been handled by the young and the old, by the infirm and the spunky, it takes on a whole new character. What else is there in the made world has such a life of venal, venereal, visceral splendour before it comes into contact with our own bodies? At least the cutlery in restaurants gets a good clean before we put it into our vulnerable little mouths. But money? No we handle it and touch it and carry it in all its smelly splendour. No wonder the credit card companies are cleaning up. It seems that we need the surety and the distance that the credit card gives us. We need that cleanliness. You consumers out there. Imagine if you actually had to come up with the money, the hard cash, before you bought the car or the tv or the stereo, or worse, the house. Imagine the wheelbarrow full of dirty, smelly money you would have to trundle up the garden path. Imagine that and then ask yourself if you would ever bother buying anything, at all, ever. It is all exchange, you see, and if we took the full weight of responsibility for our symbols of exchange, then we

would have to address certain fundamental problems to do with the inadequacy of our thinking in terms of value and meaning and how we assess and measure the worth of what we do in our work and in our lives. At the moment we assess the value of economic exchange via the idea of money and this is the dominant ideology in the world of late capitalism. As such the dominant ideology has the power to hegemonise and affect everything that surrounds it or comes into contact with it. The problem that we have to address is that everything we do, we do for the principle of exchange, either for money or honour or value or the self. There are few acts, few states which escape the laws of exchange, where we commodify the results of our ability to abstract, to think and to make. This is

partly a problem of intertextuality, of modernity and the burden of knowledge which we cynical and worldly citizens of late capitalism are forced to carry. Late capitalism: there's an idea to conjure with. The dying rays of this civilisation, the late phase of this part of our development where to civilise is to commodify is to trade: where to be is to exchange. Where capital – money, the potential of money – continually hegemonises our relationship to what we do and who we are, where we are and where we want to be. And late capitalism implies in its name the finality of our phase, we're nearly finished, it says, bear with us, we are nearly there. We're nearly done with the money thing. But what next? Whatever next? If there is a way of thinking that offers an alternative to the ill-defined,

pure potential of the great postmodern bluff-fest then we need it now. I have a feeling that the answer lies in seeking authenticity in whatever way we can find it, the goal: the recognition of the real as a state of being and of thinking. Eschew the fake and the false in favour of the authentic in what we do and say and suddenly the possibility of the next phase becomes entirely positive. Think in terms of honesty and authenticity in our intentions and our acts and suddenly I can't wait for late capitalism to be over and done with. Capitalism is a spent force. Be it late or otherwise, with its reliance on the ownership of the symbol of wealth – of money – which in itself has no direct structuralist link to anything of real value (we are not even on a gold standard, or any common standard anymore and haven't been for some time, money is simply valued against itself) capital and capitalism have been shown to corrupt the lives of all those who are involved with them. In truth, it is unlikely that this system will disappear and be replaced with another way in a simple linear progression. But there is potential in developing the antidote to the unauthentic qualities of the trade in meaningless symbols of monetary wealth. This will have to be a simultaneous condition: the acknowledgement of birth and death, the thrownness into life that we all experience, being there – wherever that is – in the moment with an eye on our past and hope for the future, looking for love and trust and hope, and finding it under the ancient light of long dead stars.

CONVERSATION NUMBER THREE.

flowers so satisfy our desire for colour and beauty, that

we cannot imagine a world without them.

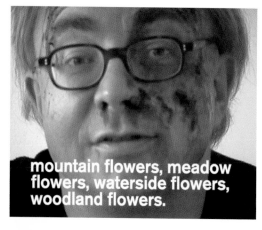

mountain flowers, meadow flowers, waterside flowers, woodland flowers.

we live in a beautiful garden that is filled with sunlight .

and laughter. (laughter).

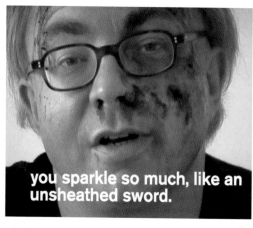

you sparkle so much, like an unsheathed sword.

a really good sword should remain in its sheath.

where do you live ? (shouts).

i live everywhere, i am a wanderer, i roam your planet.

you are beautiful. (laughs).

yes i am.

she is so beautiful.

(she flicks back her hair).

you are like the wind, you are life itself.

i am wind.

i am life.

silent, eternal.

he is entrapt.

i am lost in our garden, i cannot find the path.

i am the path.

THE END.

I REMEMBER BEING SURPRISED BY HOW WARM, SOFT AND

WET IT FELT.
IT SEEMED LIKE THIS MOMENT THIS VERY SECOND WAS
THE MOST PERSONAL AND TRUSTING MOMENT WE HAD SPENT
TOGETHER.

MY FINGERS MOVED SLOWLY AND GENTLY INSIDE HER,
MY EYES WATCHING HER FOR ANY SIGN.
I COULD NOT THINK OF ANY SENSATION I HAD EXPERIENCED
EQUAL TO THIS.
I REMEMBER BRIEFLY THE IMAGE OF WET FLOWER PETALS
ENTERING MY HEAD.

I ONCE SAW A WHITE LIGHT.
I SAW WHAT SEEMED TO BE AN EXTREMELY LARGE AMOUNT
OF WHITE LIGHT IN AN EXTREMELY SHORT AMOUNT OF
TIME.
THE AMOUNT OF LIGHT IN THE AMOUNT OF TIME IS

SIGNIFICANT.
THE MEANING OF THE WHITE LIGHT I COULD NOT
FULLY EXPLAIN.

I REMEBER A FEELING AS IF WE WERE FALLING
INTO ONE ANOTHER.
THE FALL WAS BOTH SUDDEN AND ENDLESS.

IT WAS AS IF EVERY CELL IN OUR BEING BECAME
MAGNIFIED AN INFINITE NUMBER OF TIMES.
I BECAME AT ONCE FORMLESS BUT AT THE SAME TIME
SUPER CONCENTRATED.
TIME MOVED SLOWLY, SECONDS SEEMED TO ALLOW

HUNDREDS OF SEPERATE FULLY FORMED AND CLEAR
THOUGHTS TO OCCUR.

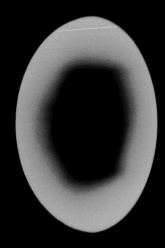

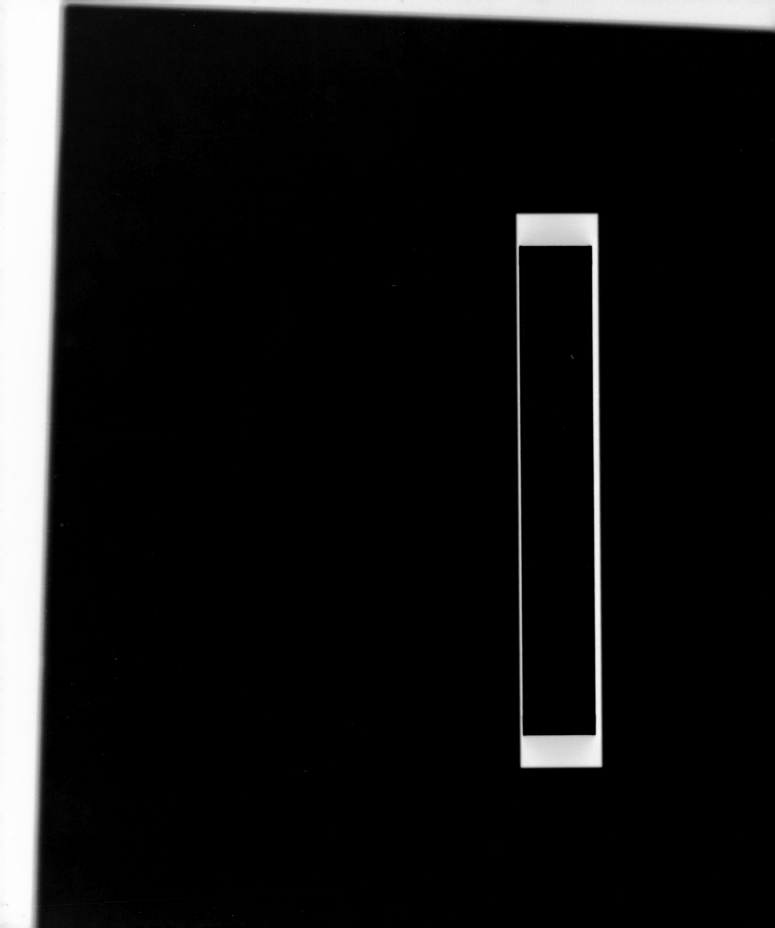

"Ichiban" was the only word she said In boy's bar near Aoyama Dori But she said it again and again and Again, so I knew it must mean something To her if not to me, because, i speak No japanese. Boy's bar at five in the morning feels like No other place on the face of the earth And the girl that had followed us from blue Was dressed in thin clothes and looked so good. And daylight was coming through the windows In Tokyo. The one way conversation continued "Ichiban", yes, she said it once again. Blinded by beer and wine and time I knew Nothing, least of all her japanese name. She existed then more like an idea But real and near. Now it's six o'clock in the morning and She's as pissed as me. I've got a plane To catch at eight from Narita Airport. She gently cups my face and kisses me. "Goodbye 'Ichiban,'" she says for fun, "it Means: 'Number one.'"

Reading Heart of Darkness on a bus through Aberfan. A child is playing on the street of mean little houses. Later, on the Train a woman who's dressed in lilac Velour talks incessantly of her own America: where she's from, and where she wants to be herself. To be her Reading That's Life, Zest and Take A Break, too, She's leaning on her hand and on the back Of it she has written the number of A man. The train is going to London, We are moving east, rushing toward "my" Europe in the strangest company. And Then we start to slow down until we are Almost imperceptibly moving, still, And a voice comes over the speakers and Says "I'm sorry that the train cannot go Any faster, but we have been told that There are children playing on the railway Line. We can't go any faster, in case..." But he will not finish the sentence now, And so as the train begins to pick up Speed, we all start to imagine the worst.

Here it comes, in from the north east, in from Amsterdam way or the German Bight, Across The downs and onto the marshes; Yet another belt of grey rain, in from The sea to dampen the shingle, wet the Stones and fill the puddles. This is a cold Rain driven by a Baltic wind and it Falls on the earth; the loamy marsh drinks its Fill. But, there in the distance, sodium Arc lights blazing, whistling and humming is The nuclear pile. Atoms entombed in grey-streaked old Concrete are now decaying in discrete Proportion to themselves. And in the half Light of dusk the unimaginable Stillness of their power unsettles me And makes me wish for another day when perhaps the sun is Shining and there is little in view save For the sea, the sky and the horizon.

Imagine a big ship working the Po or the Tiber two thousand years ago. Imagine the cargo the spices, the lambs, The glassware, the fine grained sand, Think of the Mediterranean sun Upon the Mediterranean sea. Then, imagine if you can, the day the Orders came that were to send him to the Northernmost part of the empire: to Grain, To Thanet and Sheppey. To the flat wild Essex marshes, where a captain like him Could not imagine such cold and such damp, Plying a river the colour of lead Under a sky that looks like gunmetal. Imagine the difference he travels Every night when he goes to his bed And remembers the place that he came from, And curses the Thames and Londoners dead.

I have tried to manufacture just a small space, Lacuna or hiatus, in which words can form Themselves. Born, as they are in silence and at night, Or in the daylight, they find their form when I speak. If I do not speak them, the words, nevertheless, Keep their form. How they achieve this, I do not know.

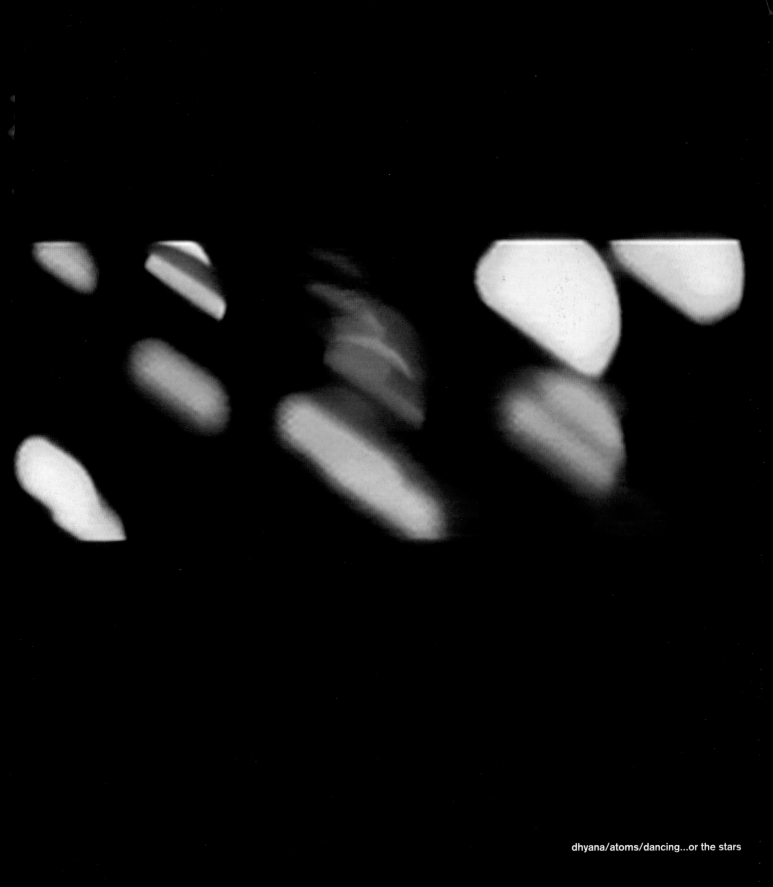

dhyana/atoms/dancing...or the stars

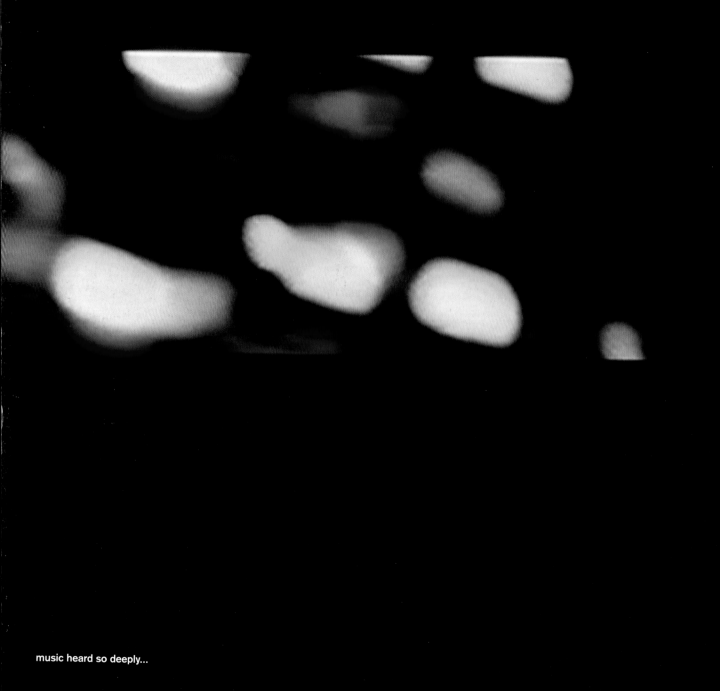

music heard so deeply...

...that it is not heard at all

dhyana om dhyana...

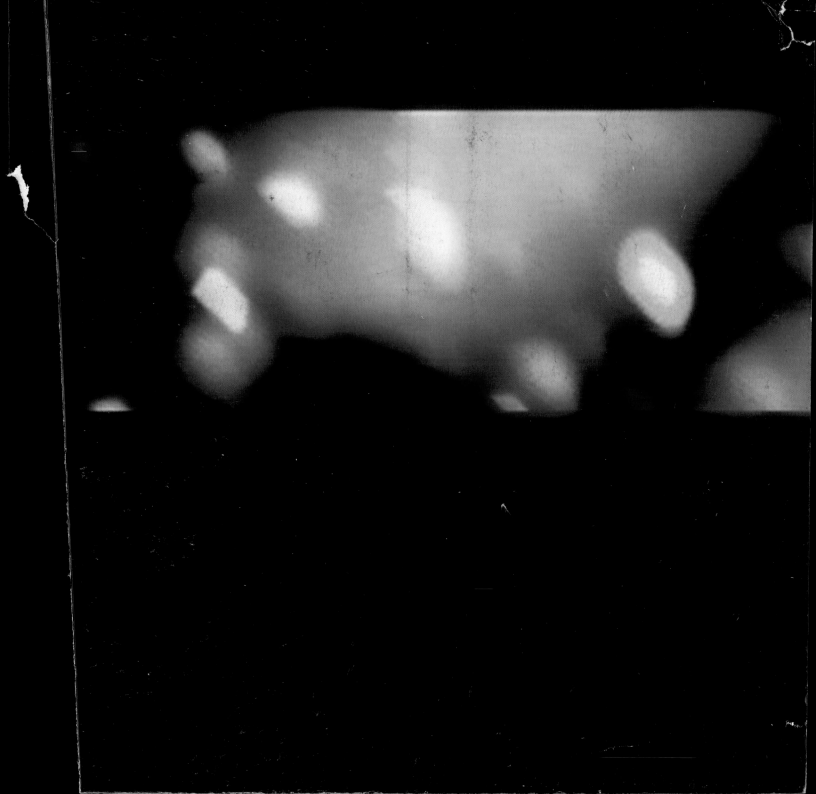